GUNNERS GET GLORY

THE ARMED GUARD WATCH IS SET

GUNNERS GET GLORY

Lt. Bob Berry's Story of the Navy's Armed Guard

AS TOLD TO

LLOYD WENDT
Co-author with Herman Kogan
of *Lords of the Levee*

●●●

THE BOBBS-MERRILL COMPANY
Publishers

INDIANAPOLIS   NEW YORK

THE CORNWALL PRESS, INC., CORNWALL, N. Y.

To the
Officers and Men
of the
Naval Armed Guard Crews
Aboard Merchant Ships
in Time of War

Contents

List of Illustrations

GUNNERS GET GLORY

Foreword

BOB BERRY is not a letter-writing man and I had kept track of his peregrinations only by a kind of elemental grapevine that is available to newspapermen and laundresses. When I came to my office shortly after the outbreak of war and saw Bob's scrawl across a big white envelope addressed to me, I knew it was something of unusual importance and immediately guessed its nature. Bob was shoving off. A few months before, when I had last seen him, he was hot for the Army, but this letter came from Norfolk. Bob had sniffed the salt air again, and I remembered with considerable nostalgia that summer when we cruised the coast in an old model-T Ford and the seafarin' urge first struck us landlubbers from the Dakota plains. We tried to ship on a fruit steamer then, and almost made it, but at that time there were three of us, and one of us three, who were bound together by an inviolable oath, had a girl friend out West . . . but that is another story. We didn't ship that time. We helped build a dam near Albany instead, and then, using discarded brake bands and with bacon rinds in our bearings, we enticed our old flivver back to South Dakota and college. It was the next Halloween, incidentally, that the flivver was placed on the dais of the college chapel, but neither Bob nor I, obviously, had anything to do with that.

13

"I've got to get in this show," Bob wrote. "We waited too long, and I've waited too long. I don't know a damned thing about the sea, but they're not asking so many questions now, and maybe I can learn. I just want one shot at the people who have messed up this world. Will you write me at . . . ?"

In Navy school Bob was too busy to write. Then came a cryptic telegram from New York. "DETLIE'S DOWN UNDER." That I knew. Master Sergeant Harold "Nuts" (he liked pecans) Detlie, who once held down the stern sheets of our jalopy with a rugged girth that later plowed a good many holes through the Dakota conference lines, had sailed off to the South Pacific with the Army many weeks before. Bob, I gathered, expected to see him.

Next I learned, by grapevine, that Bob had been torpedoed and cast up on a southern coast, after many harrowing adventures. Soon it was said that he was at sea again. Then came the report that he was missing. But this was an error. His ship had been sunk, he was rescued, and sunk again. He finally showed up aboard a life raft, so the story went, losing never an ounce by the experience. Then I heard that Bob had been cited for bravery under fire, in addition to other commendations that had come his way. I sent an urgent message: "Why in hell don't you write?" I was in the newspaper business, and here was one of the finest news stories of the year gallivanting up and down the high seas, with never an effort on Berry's part to put a hard-working friend in touch with a good thing.

Finally I got off to Navy school myself. One day I got two letters, one from Bob Berry, the other from Nuts Detlie. They were 12,000 miles apart when they wrote. "Hey," said Nuts. "I hear that guy Berry has been down here." "Just got back," wrote Bob. "I almost got down to where Detlie is. And what the devil are you doing? I hear you were in New York last week. I looked for you, but New York is a big place. We gotta get together. I hear you wrote a book. Boy, I could write one too, if only I wrote books. Look, we can get together at Baltimore next week end."

Not even a war can keep a newspaperman from setting down a story when it comes his way by such sheer good luck. This story, of course, is Bob Berry's. He cannot be held accountable for the actual words, for I, in my shore seclusion, strung them out of nights while Bob was banging away at enemy subs. And our good wives, Anne Berry and Helen Wendt, did the yeoman work. But it's Bob's story, and when it catches up with him, somewhere on the high seas, I think he'll find it much the story we weaned from him, bit by bit, between sailings.

First, I think you may want to know a bit more about Bob, for he utters little that is personal in his narrative of the Armed Guard. I first met him when he was coming out of high school in Sioux Falls, South Dakota, back in 1926.

I had graduated the day before from a school in a little town in the hinterlands, and had come up to Sioux Falls to work for a daily paper. One of my first assignments was to get a story on the high-school dance, and Bob, I discovered, was running it.

He was, in fact, running just about the entire graduation program. I took a preconceived dislike for this paragon of high-school leadership who seemed to be a one-man commencement week. Then I met him. He lurched toward me with a big wide grin, his sandy hair jutting down over one eye, his tux looking as though it had been slept in, a big, warm paw shoved out—and we were friends.

Bob was a kind of hero to me from there on in. He was, I noted in the press clippings, president of the Associated Young Peoples' Societies in Sioux Falls. He was the master of a Scout troop. He operated a gym class for underprivileged boys. He played baseball. He knew all the girls in town. He was summoned to grave conferences with ministers and Y men and civic-club presidents, and yet, of a night, he raised more hell than anyone I had ever known. I was a small-town lad, stranger in the city (population 35,000), and Bob Berry took me in. I was his guy. For me, it was a kind of high-school postgraduate crush, and all I asked was for the dear Lord to let me emulate Bob Berry.

Bob wanted to attend medical school at the state university, but instead, because of his stringent financial situation, he had to remain at home and work his way through college. My position on the staff of a morning newspaper afforded me daylight hours for the pursuit of education. Together we selected the Baptist school on the south end of the town, Sioux Falls College. It was I who nominated Bob for president of the Freshman class. The groundwork had been laid among the out-of-town students by those good friends and archconspirators, Jimmy Deacon and Bud Hahn, upperclassmen who were not above taking hand in a yearling election. The Sioux Falls contingent of course backed Bob to a man. He was elected.

In college none of us did especially well. Bob worked in a department store uptown, and most of the rest of the students with equal necessity, held down jobs while firmly refusing to let studies interfere with the few social hours that remained. Anyhow, we had a good time, although, during football season, Bob elected to work till midnight in the stock room of the store so he could go out for practice. He made the scrub eleven, which at the time seemed to him, and to me, an incomparable achievement.

At some time during the Freshman year, Mother Berry, plump, jolly, and an unequaled expert with Southern fried spring chicken, decreed that since Bob and I were together most of our waking time, I might as well come out and live with them. So, during many of the few hours that remained to us to sleep, we plotted school politics, fought over girls (invariably we chose the same beauty), and cast the future of the world. Bob was the idealist, the dreamer. He was religious, in a way, and loved justice. He wanted a just world. We worried over Plato and Spinoza and Hobhouse and Wundt but organized a very satisfactory universe without too much trouble. We talked endlessly of sports. Bob, who could have won a school popularity contest hands down, passionately desired instead to Play on the Team. That first fall he was mighty happy with the scrubs. The second year he smashed his knee. It was an injury that made him morbidly distrustful of his luck, and at the same time gave him enormous satisfaction. At least it was honorably acquired. Occasionally—that is, frequently—we talked about Women and Sex. We were purists and idealists. More young men are than most persons suspect.

It was during the winter of our Freshman year that we organized a dance band, the Venetians. None of us has ever been able to remember just how or why we chose that name. It was not a very good dance band. I remember that George Talbott, columnist on the local morning paper, commented that the music we played into the instruments was sweet enough, but that something horrible happened before it came out again. Anyhow, the band was in great demand, and we toured the state. The next year we toured again, but that time as a Gospel Team, which had the unanimous approval of the Baptist fathers of the school. We found that we could date the same girls en tour and we had the additional satisfaction of church chicken suppers. The Gospel Team experience was the forerunner of the sermons Bob has delivered to his faith-hungry men at sea, a possibility we then would have considered fantastic.

Neither Bob nor I had ever seen a Big City, so, at the end of our Freshman year, we boarded an excursion train for Chicago. Our notable successes in establishing the whereabouts of Riverview Park without police aid, and trekking the five miles from the YMCA to the Uptown Theater (we had looked out a twentieth-floor window and concluded the Uptown was a few blocks away in the Loop), inspired in us a lust for travel. The next year we purchased a 1913 Ford, rebuilt it ourselves, and started off on a tour of the East. We slept in the open, ate bananas on the Capitol steps, tried to ship out of Baltimore, and finally got a job mucking on a dam near Albany. Then a strike was called, and we were shooed off the premises toward home.

Thereafter our paths split. Bob went off to the University of Minnesota, and I enrolled at Northwestern. Bob wanted to be a doctor. Hundreds of times he told me the story of the Kentucky physician who had saved his life when he was a boy in the Southern hills. Bob wanted to be a country doctor. That, to him, was the Good Life. He was sorry that doctors no longer drove about in buggies.

At Christmastime we both raced back to Sioux Falls to flash our stuff at the Pan-Hellenic. During the summers our association renewed. But Bob was unhappy. He didn't have the funds for a medical education, and he changed to busi-

ness administration instead. Finally we were both graduated, we celebrated in Chicago, and returned to Sioux Falls
to jobs. Bob headed a department in a downtown department store; I was telegraph editor of the *Daily Argus-
Leader*.

One day Bob walked in. "I'm going to medical school,"
he said.

"Have you got the money?"

"No. There must be some way to get through. Look at
all the people who need doctors. I don't care how I do it.
I don't care whether I ever make any money"—he was doing
all right at the store—"I'm going to be a doctor . . . out there
among the farms. I figure you just live in this world to do
some good, and that's the best way I can think of to do it."

Bob went to the University of South Dakota. I returned
to graduate school at Northwestern and then obtained a
Chicago newspaper job. We didn't bother to write. One
day Bob popped in.

"I got my premedic," he announced. "I had to stay out
and work, but I did it. Now I'm going to school here."

But in those years, it was said, there were too many doctors. The schools couldn't admit a man without a certain
amount of money. Bob had to give up. He refused to return to business. He elected schoolteaching as second best
and went to North Dakota. Very shortly he was second in
command of the adult educational program for the state.

The next time I saw Bob, he was bound for the East. We were no longer schoolboys. And we were now genuinely worried about the future of the world.

"You going into service?" Bob demanded.

"I suppose so. When do you go?"

"Soon as the damn Army quits being so particular. They claim they've got too many men. I wish to heaven I had some military experience."

Neither of us spoke of the Navy. We had been too close to the land to think of ships and the sea. But a few months later the Japs struck, and then I got the letter from Bob. He was married, to Anne, and she was swell, but he had to go in.

Anne told me about it later. It was an early December evening and Bob and Anne were in Pittsburgh, her home town, and were parked on a hill overlooking the mills where you can see the Ohio, Allegheny and Monongahela marking the boundaries of the city. Up and down the three rivers the mills stretched, belching flame and thick, black smoke, darker than the night, and Bob told her:

". . . It's part of what we've got and what we've got to keep. I wish every fellow in the United States could knock around as I have so he could see how big it all is and how he is only one little part of it and maybe not worth much in himself, but together it's all worth keeping. I wish we'd all quit being tied up with our thinking of ourselves and our own little group. Someday we'll have to fight to keep what we have and to give the good of what we've got to those who need it. We'll have to fight and that means that the little part of it that's me . . . I've got to get into it. . . ."

Then came Pearl Harbor, and the next day Bob went down to the recruiting office again and they didn't ask so many questions.

This is Bob Berry's story, but it is not necessarily a story about Bob Berry. He has no patience with heroics. He is doing no more than millions of other men and women. He is simply finishing a job denied him when he couldn't become a country doctor. He is doing a bit of good by fighting a great evil that is in the world. This is a story about the Navy's Armed Guard, and the merchantmen who carry men and supplies to our bases throughout the world. Supplies. That gentle word includes dynamite and TNT and oil and innumerable other inflammables that burst out into the blackness of roaring waters and lowering night when a tin fish stabs the bowels of a wallowing freighter. This is a story of watches and drills and wet and danger and cold and hunger and the courage and sacrifice of men who want at least one shot at those who have messed up a peaceful world. In the Armed Guard the gunners frequently get in their best shooting when they are down by the stern and the decks are awash and the submarine emerges to unlimber her deck gun for the *coup de grâce*. There is heroism, heroism aplenty, but it is the quiet stuff of the service. Bob Berry's experiences are the experiences of many hundreds of men. This is a story of the Armed Guard.

LLOYD WENDT

Part I

ATLANTIC

1

WHEN it happens it happens so quickly you can't tell afterward whether all the things you feared and expected were a part of it. You were scared, scared as hell, you remember that, but it was not the kind of fear you lived through all those dark nights of the watches, for it was something never before a part of your experience, and something you couldn't anticipate. All the little personal fears concerning how you would act in a jam, and whether you would come through, and whether something inside you couldn't help would let you down—those things that looked so big up to the time disappeared completely. You just did the necessary things without thinking about it, you had an overwhelming awe for the men around you who came through with such grim calmness, and a terrible pity for those few poor wretches who cracked. You knew suddenly that there is nothing to fear but fear itself. Phobophobia . . . but the term escaped you then. You struggled in the black water thinking absolutely that you were in the hands of God, and your faith was enormous. You did the right thing without thinking. And then, when it came, the blast and hurtling flame licking out at you, the glare searing the waves, the little blobs of flotsam and rafts dancing crazily away from you, you stopped feeling altogether and there was nothing left but an empty numbness and your heart burning and slamming against your ribs.

The things you remember most clearly are not those final, fatal minutes at the gun, when you are sinking by the bow and the decks are awash and you wait for the conning tower to show for one final blast at him before it's over; nor the rushing of men and the bawling of orders nor the rattle of the buzzers as the cry comes: "All hands prepare to abandon ship!" nor the scramble for the boats as she lurches to port, nor even the first welcome sight of the patrol plane that will, God help us, mark the position. What I remember are things like that morning we hauled Gallegos, second-class seaman, aboard after we had gone down in the South Atlantic.

Faustin Gallegos was one of those lean, grinning Southerners who come out of the hills of Tennessee and grow to such amazing height in the warm suns of Florida. He hadn't done much thinking about the war until it started and then he thought the thing to do was get in and fight. Gallegos hadn't done much thinking about the Navy either, but he figured that the Navy would be where the fighting was thickest. So he wound up in my crew of the Armed Guard.

When Gallegos discovered, the second day out, that we might cruise the seven seas without ever firing a shot, he grew bored. He grew permanently sleepy as well, and, while his big grin and his chuckle always were around when we needed them most, it got so we began to give him the little chores, leaving the more serious business of the war to those who were more aggressive. We loved our thin-shanked Gallegos, every one of us, but we despaired of ever making a sailor of him. I figured that when trouble came he would do his job passing well and that was as much as I had a right to expect. No amount of pep talk nor threats fazed him. We had to take Gallegos for what he was, and that, we thought then, was a little short of what the *Blue-jackets' Manual* contemplated.

When the fish caught us and the ship blew up I didn't know whether Gallegos got clear or not. I was wrapped up in a telephone line at the time, and I didn't see him aboard, but the mere fact that he probably jumped into the sea when the lifeboat at his starboard station was crushed, by no means reassured me. After that I was too busy to worry about anyone not in sight and I must admit that I had given little thought to Gallegos and his possible fate by the time we were picked up the following day. Then two boats and a raftload of us were rescued, and there was no sign of him. It was not until early that evening, when we had given the men medical attention, received dry clothing, and returned on deck, that another "floating object" was sighted.

As we drew abeam the floating object the skipper handed me his glasses. I looked. I counted sixteen men, and there, sitting aft on a pile of duffel, was Faustin Gallegos. He had one hand on an oar he was using as a kind of tiller, the other was hauling a line evidently secured to a drogue, or sea anchor. In his teeth was a gleaming knife.

I heard the story later.

Gallegos had been thrown clear of the wreckage, and had managed to swim away from the spreading flame. He saw an empty life raft, made for it, pulled himself aboard, and then, guided by shouts and the light of our burning ship, he managed to propel the raft through the sea until he had picked up three men.

These men he put to work as a crew. Like him, they had not been to sea before, and they were scared. Most of all they feared the sub. They had heard stories of U-boats that machine-gun survivors, and that sub was most certainly shelling the ship and whatever happened to be near her.

"Listen," Gallegos told them. "Where in hell would you guys be if all I thought about was gettin' th' hell outen here? There's more guys around here, just like me an' you, and we're pickin' 'em up."

Our ship went under, and the blackness of the night got as thick and wet as the sea itself. But still Gallegos kept them rowing. They picked up three men, then three more, and then there were sixteen of them. The raft was jammed with wet, chattering, exhausted sailors and those first saved were ready to drop at their oars.

Someone, no one remembers who, set up a clamor for the whisky and provisions aboard.

"Git out th' rations," ordered a voice. "Git us th' whisky!

By God, it's a wonder a man can live in a night like this. I'm cold to th' bone. Break out that whisky!"

Gallegos had the emergency rations and gear up under his legs. He also had in his belt a heavy hunting knife he found in the emergency box.

"We ain't drinkin' no rations," he told them. "God knows how long this stuff has gotta last. Our job now is to row, an' row like hell. I'm skippering this mattress. Now, you men turn to th' oars and give those boys a lift."

"I'm not rowin' without I eat something."

"I ain't rowin' without I got somethin' warm in my belly."

"By God!" cried Gallegos. "You all don't row and you'll git this hasp in your belly! Now, pull to port there. We gonna go westward."

"Westward! How in hell do you know which way is westward?"

"Jeez," said Gallegos. "You think I hunted all my life 'thout knowin' where th' North Star is? I got it figured. Lay to them oars, men."

Through that long night he kept them at it. There were men aboard who backed him up, but when others grew too scared and cold to think of anything but their hunger, Gallegos brandished the knife and yelled at the top of his voice:

"I'm skipper here, you sons-of-bitches! We gotta row. We gotta save them rations. Now row, you bastards, row!"

By morning they were all half dead from battling the sea, and Gallegos was sitting there with his knife in his teeth, heading her into the waves and figuring how he would issue rations. Then they sighted us.

When they came alongside the Navy patrol boat that had just saved the rest of us, Gallegos was no longer seeing anything. He just sat there, staring forward, the knife still in his teeth, and they said he was still muttering in his throat: "Row, you bastards! Row, you bastards! Row!"

That morning, with the sky sodden and the gray sea boiling and Faustin Gallegos sitting there in the raft on the pile of duffel with the knife in his teeth . . . that is one of the things I am never going to forget.

2

There were ten of us, and we were going down to the sea. In our pockets were bright new sheafs of communications from the Bureau of Navigation, which in the beginning acknowledged that we had all been duly commissioned officers in the United States Naval Reserve and in the end commanded us to present ourselves for temporary duty under instruction at the Armed Guard school. Not many casual observers would have suspected our condition as officers and gentlemen by Act of Congress, nor, certainly, our ultimate destination: the Armed Guard. We did not look like Armed Guards. We looked more like delegates to a convention of the Junior Chamber of Commerce, except that four of us, not including myself, were unmistakably in the uniform of the United States Navy. Marsh, that is, was partly in such a uniform. The cap he had forgotten in a restaurant, a situation that didn't worry him half enough, for he hadn't yet seen a copy of Navy Regulations. It is a far more grievous offense to be part out of uniform than to be out of uniform completely.

There were ten of us—a schoolmaster, a salesman, a business executive, an auto mechanic, a stock raiser and five others, none of us youths, most of us leaving wives somewhere, and some of us leaving children. We were among the first of the Armed Guards, and already it had become a service many sensible men were avoiding.

We were pretty happy as we debarked for what previously had been described as the gate of the school at Little Creek, for we felt that exciting adventure lay ahead of us, and the weight of leave-taking we had already pushed aside.

The gate, we discovered, was a kind of sentry box, which was under the supervision of a petty officer, placed there evidently for the very purpose of receiving such newly commissioned persons as ourselves.

The CPO, his sleeve heavy with hash marks, looked us over as we swung our baggage up the road. He noted Marsh and the six of us out of uniform with special disfavor.

"Reporting for duty?" he inquired.

"Yes, sir," we replied in chorus, fishing for our orders. "Armed Guard." We didn't know then that the CPO was from the Inshore Patrol, which at the time had its own ideas about the Armed Guard, ideas somewhat influenced by the fact that the Guard proposed to take over part of the barracks the Patrol had built for itself.

The CPO looked at Marsh. "Where's your cap?" he demanded.

"Lost," said Marsh, suddenly aware he had committed some sort of offense, the exact nature of which still eluded him.

"Landlubbers!" snorted the CPO. He was having his day. He looked at the rest of us. "Reporting for active duty out of uniform!" These remarks preceded his inspection of our orders. Having convinced himself that we were actually officers, on paper at least, the CPO drew himself up stiffly and saluted the four in uniform who promptly returned four of the sloppiest salutes I have ever seen.

"Office in the barracks directly ahead, sir," he said to Marsh. His accent on "sir" demonstrated the wonderfully damning effect an idea can have on a word.

"I'd swear I heard son-of-a-bitch in it somewhere," Marsh said as we moved up the road.

The barracks were three big rambling structures a quarter of a mile from the gate. They loomed dully against the yellow clay that stretched everywhere and they made me think of tobacco barns, rather than structures designed for human habitation. Mac, the fellow from California, groaned as he looked them over.

"Jeez," Mac said, "I signed up for a ship. Look at that clay. They're going to make us *walk* on it. They wouldn't have that much clay around without some purpose behind it. And you know what's going to happen? It will rain, and this will be yellow gumbo, up to our elbows, and then they will have us *walk* in that! And then that damn CPO will get out pup tents and they will have us sleep in it. Dammit, I signed up for a ship and the first thing I have to do is sleep in the mud."

Mac grumbled all the way up to the barracks. It was the only time in all the days I knew him that he ever uttered a

35

word in criticism of the Navy. From then on in, to hear Mac, you'd think that the Armed Guard was a kind of official heaven opened up for his special benefit. But evidently the look the CPO had given him got under his skin.

I had to admit that the gate reception and the appearance of the place weren't any too cheering. But I had seen the Creek before. Six months before the grounds had been a marsh. The only thing there then was the ferry dock and a couple of fishing shacks and a hot-dog stand and an oyster bar along the road. Since that time the Navy had been busy dragging in the clay, while the Inshore Patrol built barracks for the men who did the first job of patrolling in their little converted yachts and fishing boats. The three buildings they had put up, desolate and ominous, appearing completely unrelated to the little group of men who were drilling on the flatlands in the distance, didn't much improve the scene.

We dragged our baggage through the dust, reached a doorway labeled HEADQUARTERS and cautiously pushed inside to present our orders. I was scared then, scared as I have ever been since. I had my orders and my commission with a stripe and a half in my pocket, but I was a landlubber, as the CPO had pointed out, and I knew it. My first salute was worrying me more than my first day at sea did later. Did you salute in civilian clothes? Did you salute inside? I didn't know. I wanted passionately to do things right, to live up to Navy traditions I knew nothing about,

ATLANTIC

and that first day I would have walked a mile in Mac's
gumbo rather than run the risk of making some minor mistake. Funny, the way we put values on things.

Inside the barracks we joined a group of other men and
spent the next several minutes looking suspiciously at one
another, each of us willing that someone else should make
the initial move and learn about Navy ways first. Finally a
headful of curly red hair poked out of a doorway down the
corridor, and a voice called out: "You men reporting for
active duty?"

"Yes, sir!" we yelled again.

"Well, then, forward march!" the voice commanded, and
a sailor with a rating stripe on his sleeve emerged from the
doorway, grinning at his chance to give orders to a group of
officers with commissions in their pockets. We marched up.
"Stow your gear against this bulkhead," the sailor directed,
indicating a wall.

There was not much to presenting our orders, we discovered. We watched the OD affix the 1330 stamp, and were
happy at least to be able to figure Navy time. Then a new
CPO swung out, ordered us into formation with our bags,
and called us to attention. The orders began cracking:
"About . . . face! Forward . . . harch! Hup two three
four, hup two three four."

The CPO didn't waste any time teaching us. "All right,
men, get on the beat! Hup two three four. Hup two three
four. Get your eyes off the deck! . . . Keep your eyes in

37

the boat! Hup two three four. Hup two three four. Column riiide, harch!"

We made it. I looked at Mac. He grinned at me. Happiness had descended upon him. We hit a stride, on the beat, and a feeling of exultation made my blood tingle. Already, those barracks were looking good. We had got our teeth into something, we didn't yet know just what, but we swung with the easy cadence and it felt good to be in the Navy.

We entered another barracks door, identical with the first except that it bore no headquarters sign, and the CPO shouted to us:

"All right, men, you did well. Some of you men are going topside. Remember to hit them ladders on th' double. Don't crowd th' ladders, men. Hit 'em on the double."

The ladders, we judged, were the stairs. We hit them on the double. It was a phrase we were to hear endlessly in the Navy, and we finally discovered its true meaning when Battle Stations sounded at sea. I suppose, when the war is over, there will be millions of men about the world who will go on hitting the ladders on the double. You can't get over it. A stairway challenges you.

We were glad to be barracked together, the ten of us. Somehow we felt that we were already friends. Inside our quarters we dropped our bags and took a good look at one another.

Mac put out his hand. "I'm MacKenzie," he said.

A long, thin, sad-eyed Southerner stepped up. "Ah'm Jackson."

"I'm Berry. Glad to know you."

A fourth member of our group, a big-shouldered, slim-waisted man who balanced a heavy frown on thick black eyebrows, was prowling about the room. He raised up to take part in the formalities. "Ah'm Caldwell," he announced, rivaling Jackson in his rich accent. "Ah'm God-damned if this ain't a hole." He grinned appreciatively.

We looked about the room. A bare floor, a few desks and chairs, a bare electric bulb overhead.

"Wheah do we sleep?" asked Caldwell.

"In heah," said Jackson softly. He was inspecting the bunks in a tiny alcove, just big enough to contain ten of them. "My heavens, all of us goin' a sleep in heah?"

Outside the mate of the deck was shouting something. "Mustah th' first platoon! Mustah th' first platoon on first deck. Mustah on first deck. Ona double!"

"That's us," Mac said.

We rushed into the corridor and to the stairs. "Double ona ladders!" yelped the mate. "Double ona ladders!"

On first deck we milled through the corridor with other men while the CPO shouted orders. "Fall in, men! Fall in! Look alive there! Fall in."

We fell in, forming ranks down the corridor. The CPO, a little red-faced man with four hash marks on his sleeve, mounted a step and looked us over. "All right, men," he said. "I'm gonna teach you how to salute."

39

3

Mac is a little curly-haired guy from California and the love I bear the Navy I cheerfully credit to men like him. There is something about those first days in the barracks that welds men together. It isn't just the discipline, the routine, the marching cadence, nor even the fact that everyone on the station is part of a team striving for the same goal—though those are powerful influences. Swinging down company street in a marching column you have the exhilarating sense that you are one with an unstoppable gang that could tromp down a tank, if one came in the way. Running through gun drill you feel as if all the crew and the gun itself and even the belching shot are part of you. But it's more than that. You get to know men those first days in the barracks, while you make the break from civilian life, and in a few days you feel you've lived with them a lifetime. These close, tough, war-made friendships last—you never forget those men of the first days, whatever your experience since may be. You soon begin to get the idea that you and your friends can whip anything on earth. You know that those around you are men you can depend on; that the life of the individual means nothing and the life of the outfit is all that counts. Maybe it's the traditions and drill, but I have a feeling it's because there are always guys like Mac around, and because barracks life brings out the Mac in all of us.

It was Mac who taught me to shuck my civilian gear and notions joyfully from the first minute of the first day, and he somehow made all the beginning discomforts of military life seem delightful and desirable. Mac wanted to fight, dammit, and he could take any kicking-around the CO could devise if it would help to get to that goal sooner. Mac is a red-whiskered fire-ball who drove speedboats up and down the West Coast and whose one desire was to pilot a PT boat. He had a standing offer for the Navy which he announced loudly, belligerently and profanely a dozen times a day: If the Navy would assign him a PT boat he would take the goddam thing into any son-of-a-bitchen spot the Navy could think of and sink anything in sight, pro-vided—provided the Navy would give him the little beauty when the war was over. "Why look . . . !" said Mac.

He would go into what could be done with a PT boat in a civilian era, raising his eyebrows and staring at you in an earnestness that always moved him to the solemnest and most mouth-filling expletives I have ever heard.

The first morning at the station I woke up with Mac standing over my bunk. "Wake up, you lousy sons-a-bitches!" he was shouting amiably. "What in hell they pay-ing you for? Shake that lead out. Look alive!"

I sat up sleepy in the darkness and then the reveille bell

sounded and the mate of the deck bellowed: "Hit th' deck, mates! Rise an' shine. Hit th' deck!"

We piled out while Mac berated us in a vocabulary that would pale a merchant bosun. We learned to love it. If Mac failed to cuss you of a morning you figured he was sore. If he said something nice you knew he was a fit candidate for sick bay. But when he blistered the bulkheads with profanity it was a sign that everything was all right in what was once the best of all possible worlds.

That first morning we learned, once and for all, what the Navy meant by that incessant command, "On th' double!" Roused from our bunks, we had two minutes to get into our gear and two more to form in company street for calisthenics. Ten minutes later we were streaking back to quarters, on the double, in order to get into the heads and complete our toilet in time to begin swabbing the deck of our quarters fifteen minutes later. There were four washbowls in the head, and two mirrors, for the twenty-four men on our corner of the deck, and Navy Regs require that every man at all times be clean-shaven. Somehow we always made it. By the time we had finished swabbing there was a five-minute warning bell before the muster for chow, so we knew, without being told, that we had to get into our uniforms "on th' double."

It was during those first few days, before we went to khaki, that we learned about those pretty white Navy collars. They're of paper, and completely unmanageable. You

Official U. S. Navy Photograph

THE ARMED GUARD EMBARKS

The Armed Guard gun crew, with full equipment, embarks for duty on a merchant ship. Each man carries his own gear.

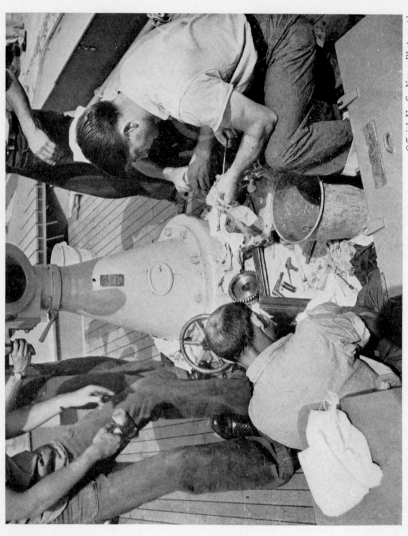

TRAINEES AT WORK ON A THREE-INCH GUN

"We dissembled and reassembled the guns until we could do it blindfolded"

have no idea what they can do to a man when the mate of the deck is mustering the company and you have two minutes to make a formation. The collars, fastened to a button aft, stand out from your neck like a pair of wings. When you pull in one side, the back pops out. When you get both tips snugly in your fingers, the tie slides down around your shoulders. Finally you hook the tie on the after collar button, wrap both ends around the front collar tabs, and then strangle with your fist between your neck and collarband while you try to force the forward button through slits cut not quite through the paper. While this is in progress the muster bell rings. That means you are to be on company street, a deck below. You force the button in desperation, grab your coat, and really make the ladders on the double.

"Muster th' second company for chow, on th' double."

Jackson couldn't make it. Collarless, he grabbed his raincoat, buttoned it snugly around his neck, and fled down the ladders. He fell in just in time.

The company officer looked us over. He shook his head in pain and fixed his eyes on Jackson.

"Collars down, men," said the CO gently.

Jackson didn't move.

"You, there!" shouted the CO. "Get that collar down."

Jackson seemed to be choking. He unfastened his raincoat collar and patted it down. There was an awful moment of silence. Then the CO couldn't restrain himself. He began to laugh. "What's your name?" he asked softly, ignoring the company chuckles.

"Jackson, suh."

"All right, Jackson, fall out. You can't go to chow without a tie, you know."

Jackson stumbled back to the barracks. "You!" cried the CO, looking at me. "Two-block that tie!"

I didn't get it. The CO demonstrated. I pulled my tie snugly to my collar. "Companie-ie-ie ten—shun!" yelled the CO. "Dress right, dress! . . . Ready . . . front . . . right face . . . forward, harch!"

We were off to chow without Jackson.

They can put a company of 250 men through a chow line in fifteen minutes: serve them, feed them, clear the trays, and muster them for the return trip to the barracks. The food is good and there is plenty of it. Cereal, toast, scrambled eggs, a strip of bacon, served on a tray with compartments that eliminate the need of dishes. While we ate we commiserated over Jackson and discussed an astounding fact. We had risen, dressed in athletic gear, taken ten minutes of calisthenics, shaved, swabbed the deck, dressed in the uniform of the day, and then marched to chow, all in the space of thirty-five minutes.

The end of our first morning chow at the Creek was also the end of what might have been called our indoctrination school training. A hurry call for Armed Guards had come from somewhere and we were the ones elected to hold the line. The officers in charge promptly threw overboard the courses designed to teach us the fine points of navigation, seamanship, naval gunnery and Naval Regulations, and we went to work at once on the guns.

That change of plans had all of us wildly excited. Ordinarily the Navy attempts to give its men at least eight weeks of training, and, if possible, more. But the scuttlebutt in the barracks was that we were going to sea in fifteen or twenty days. We were like kids at a five-ring circus, and our officers were in little better condition. We had neither the textbooks nor the equipment for streamlined training, and our education was accomplished only by the amazingly hard work of the men in the school and the consideration and devotion of the officers in charge, who knew better than we did what was ahead and who worked long hours overtime to make sure that they crammed everything possible into our heads within the limited time available.

We were supplied with quickly mimeographed instruction sheets, turned loose on the antiquated armament available, and told to learn something. We started dismantling the Brownings and Lewis guns, until we could do those jobs blindfolded. Then we worked on the loading machines, learning the routine of the gun crews. That was our first big thrill. We took battle stations around a little imitation three-incher, rammed imitation projectiles home, slammed the breech, heard the since-familiar calls: "On target . . . set . . . fire!" and caught up the casing as it was flung from the machine. It was the next thing to real target practice, and I, chief gunner's mate in my turn, with a record of shooting nothing bigger than a 16-gauge shotgun before in my life, was having the time of my life.

During our fourth day in school it was decided that the speeded-up training for officers was pointless unless we also had a supply of enlisted men in training for service with us. So we three-day wonders were given our crews, husky young sailors from boot camp, and we were told to get them ready for duty at sea.

Some of us were immediately drafted as lecturers for the enlisted men. We were to teach classes in safety precautions, procedure and customs of the Merchant Marine, the maintenance of the various guns we were to use, and eye-shooting technique. These tasks we were able to accomplish in a fashion solely by virtue of the fact that we were three days ahead of the recent boots in gunnery training and we were in possession of such instruction bulletins and manuals as were in the camp. We drilled with the men, or lectured them, all day, and sat up half the night keeping ahead of them for the morrow's lessons. The system had two advantages. We had to learn the lessons, and we found that preparing them in a way that would best permit us to communicate our discoveries to the enlisted men was a most profitable system for study. Most of us had spent years in college and university, but I doubt that any one of us learned as much in two years at college as we did in four weeks of teaching the enlisted men at the Creek.

After a few days' training with our crews we arranged time trials on loading drills. Our loading machines, which consisted of the breech and the aft part of the gun barrel mounted on a steel framework, were kept in a shed about a quarter of a mile from the barracks. Following morning chow and exercise we would double-time with our men down the cinder path to the loading shed and begin the day's run of work. A typical day would include one hour of pointing, training, and sight-setting, one hour of loading. Then we would double-time back to another shed which housed our classrooms, each slightly larger than a hall closet and almost filled by a rough pine table, plus a machine gun on its mount, and a portable blackboard. Around these objects would crowd an instructor, two officers and from ten to fifteen men. We would stand through the lecture, soaked with perspiration and grimy from our dog trot on the dusty track. Still, at each of these glorified bull sessions we managed to learn something.

After noon chow we had an hour of training film. Most of our pictures were British-made. In the beginning neither the officers nor the men could understand them. I have never been able to guess just why English is so unintelligible when it comes from a sound projector. I have met a good many Englishmen, before and since, and have never experienced the slightest difficulty in understanding our mother

47

tongue, but the training films really whipped me. We enjoyed them though, particularly the slapstick interludes
which always brought forth bursts of raucous laughter. I
don't think our British friends intended the films to be so
funny, but they frequently outdid Mack Sennett at his best,
and the boys appreciated it. We learned a lot from the pictures and we went to the visual education classes full of
curiosity and hope. Our favorite scuttlebutt always forecast
a Mickey Mouse film and we were naïvely expectant. Since
then, I understand, the Navy does use Disney's characters
to teach lessons to its fighting men.

Following the training films we had an hour's drill on
the Browning, and another hour on the Lewis gun, and, on
alternate days, an hour on spotting drill for submarines and
an hour on eye-shooting. When there was time we had
close-order drill, general lectures on naval traditions and
naval courts and boards, or a bit of work on the 20-mm.
guns.

The officers lived in the same kind of quarters as the men,
ate in the same mess hall, and took exercise with the men.
Usually one of the officer students was called upon to lead
the physical exercise each morning. I have been out to the
Creek since. They now have new quarters for men and
officers, a private officers' mess, a bar, separate apartments
for the married officers, apartments that even have rugs on
the floors. They have enlarged the classrooms, paved all the

cinder runways, have grass growing on the parade grounds, and the buildings are painted. It is almost unbelievable.

But, rugged as we thought our life at the time, we enjoyed it. And after a few days of routine study and work we arranged competitive loading matches which quickly had the entire camp in such a state of excitement we completely forgot any of the little personal discomforts attendant upon naval training life. As a matter of fact I never once heard any bitching from either a student officer or an enlisted man. We were all in deadly earnest about our work. We were very proud when our instructors wore us out physically and mentally with the heavy schedule of classes and drills. We were proud of the fact that we soft democratic Americans could take it and come back for more. We told ourselves we weren't taking half as much as the men on the firing line in Bataan and Malaysia, and, on the strength of that, we were able to come back for more.

By the end of the second week we discovered that the Navy never sets a pace it can't double every ten days. Our nerves were frayed by the grind. Even Mac seemed at the breaking point occasionally, and Jackson and Caldwell, both fresh from the calmness of law courts, dragged about with injured expressions, as if they innocently had been condemned to end their days in a madhouse.

What kept our spirits up was the boisterous good humor that broke out in horseplay just when the going seemed a little too tough. After a hard night with the books, getting ready for the next day's lectures, a good healthy explosion was had through Mac's simple expedient of spreading Grape Nuts in Caldwell's bunk. The lights went out at 2200 (ten o'clock) and the howls that went up from Caldwell when he crawled in, dead tired, gave his sadistic companions enough to go on for two more days. We were in even better condition by midweek when Caldwell retaliated by slipping a live lobster into the foot of Mac's bunk. The lobster was good and mad at having been carried in Caldwell's pocket through half a hot day, and Mac, one toe securely clamped, put on a performance that has not been equaled since Ted Kellogg dropped a lighted match inside his pajamas back at Sioux Falls College.

And then there was the time MacAllister got his shots. I didn't actually witness the incident, but I heard about it, and that was almost as good. MacAllister was a big, happy Irishman who had brought his wife to a hotel near the camp. She decided to visit him one Saturday afternoon, and that was the day we were to take our second shots. Mine were delayed because of special duty.

The Navy speeds the shots by lining up several hundred men, each stripped to the waist, who passed between the doctors and pharmacist's mates with arms akimbo so that the needles can be inserted and the shots completed, both arms at once, in a minimum of time.

MacAllister was near the head of the line, big, strapping and very impatient, for he had seen his wife drive the family flivver through the gate. The boys were ribbing him about the effect the shots would have on him (Navy men constantly suspect the Commandant of inventing new and diabolical ways of getting saltpeter into their systems) but some of the men down the line were a little gray. It is a curious but true fact that a man who will unflinchingly face cannon fire is scared to death of the inoculation needle, particularly if it happens to be in the hands of a pharmacist's mate.

Before MacAllister reached the doctor's table, he had agreed with his mates that he would faint after the ordeal and they could report to him what effect, if any, this produced on the little woman. But of course the details of the plot did not get very far down the line of shot-shy men.

MacAllister took the needles, walked three paces, and keeled over. His companions quickly seized a fire ladder hanging against the barracks, placed MacAllister aboard, and triumphantly bore him on this improvised stretcher to where Mrs. MacAllister was waiting in the car. She took one look, screeched, and fainted. This was a little more than the boys had expected. But, what was worse, the timid souls in the line had witnessed the incident without guessing that it was framed. Down the line they drooped and dropped. The doctor's day was ruined. And MacAllister nearly ran amuck until his friends pacified his wife and she agreed that he could accompany her to dinner back in town.

4

The second week we adopted Nitro, or rather Nitro adopted us. He was a little black cocker who came out of the darkness to greet us at morning muster and thereafter he never left us until we fell out at night. Nitro was more like an explosion than anything else. He was probably the happiest dog in the whole world and when he came bounding up on our flank and plowed a lane through the dust with his nose, puffing and blowing like a porpoise, he put even our commanding officer in a good humor.

Nitro liked us at first sight and went with us to chow. The results were so gratifying to him that he stuck close from then on. He joyfully led us to class, to the drill sheds, to noon and evening chow, and back to the barracks again. He gallivanted through the ranks as we mustered out, and was back as frisky as ever the next morning. Nitro got possessive. When a civilian approached he dashed out ahead of the ranks, barking fiercely, and chased the intruder away. Then he pranced proudly back, his tail fairly buzzing.

Nitro had a field day when they took the outfit's picture. He was everywhere at once during formation, and Mr. Shapiro, the photographer, was frantic.

"Get that leetle dog away from here," he begged.

But the men insisted that Nitro should be in the picture too, and the officer in charge concurred.

"But he won't stand still!" wailed Shapiro. "Git that dog outa here or there'll be no picture."

Nitro was thoroughly enjoying it. He sat demurely with the staff until Mr. Shapiro got his head under the camera curtain, and then he dashed up and down the ranks from sheer uncontrollable exuberance.

Mr. Shapiro wept. Then he cast a stone in the direction of Nitro, and the pup, untouched but horribly offended, went yelping off. Mr. Shapiro quickly snapped the picture.

The whole outfit felt tricked, and refused to buy the prints. It was not until another day, when Nitro had been cajoled into sitting still, and Mr. Shapiro had reluctantly agreed that a dog did add something to a military photograph, that satisfactory prints were produced. After that his sales were handsome.

5

Actually we had very little of formal Navy education in our streamlined Armed Guard school. There was simply no time for theory, necessary as it may be. In ordnance class, for example, we had no truck with parallax, and vector analysis, and trunnion tilt, and mooring boards and why is diphenylamine in gunpowder. They just pointed and said, "This is a four-inch gun and that is a three-inch, and if you don't believe it you can get a ruler and measure them." Then we went to work on them.

Those makeshift, overage guns became our babies. We cleaned them and bore-sighted and dissembled and reassembled and oiled and scoured until finally the CPOs, old gunnery men who could take down Navy guns in their sleep, would order us out of the place. It was necessary for us to learn our jobs without the equipment we would actually use on shipboard, for, at the time, the Navy was having trouble enough arming ships without attempting to supply the needs of the schools. We had two Oerlikons for approximately five hundred men and officers.

Of course not all our work was on the guns, even in the final days. We learned that getting your ship to the fighting and timing your operations to those of the rest of the fleet involve not only plotting and charting and star-shooting, but a sound knowledge of mathematics and astronomy. We didn't learn the work of charting and plotting or star-shooting, which are long and difficult courses in themselves, but we learned the part we would play in setting the watch bills, helping to keep station and generally taking responsibility for the security of the ship so that the navigation could go on. And we also learned that we would need an entirely new conception of time on shipboard. There is Greenwich civil time, zone time, local time, chronometer time, and watch time, not to mention the matter of hour angles, sun time, mean sun time, ship's bells and the twenty-four-hour clock.

"Jeez," said Mac, "before I got here I knew I didn't know a damn thing about sailing or guns or hydrographic charts. I couldn't tell a pelican hook from a sea painter. But I did think I could tell time. Now they've got that balled up to the point where I'll never even know what day it is."

But we were getting a whale of a kick out of everything we did, the officers in charge were splendid, the men were up to their ears in sea talk, and the only cry that interrupted work was: "When in hell are we going to get out of here and on a ship?"

Finally we got aboard one, a training ship. We went down to the coast to board her and sailed out for target practice. Everyone really went wild then. I was the senior officer in charge of the gunners on the cruise. Save for the

Navy regulars in the party, not a man, including myself, had been to sea or had handled heavy artillery.

Our rookie gun crews were assigned to regular gun stations and we worked them in gunnery drill, safety precautions, and machine-gun field stripping. After two days of this, we went on the firing range. Each gun was to fire a series of five rounds, with the officer in charge of one series plotting the range and scale and the gun captain in charge of the next series being given the opening range and allowed to carry on from there.

It was then we discovered the complexities of genuine naval gunnery. There is more to it than aiming and pulling the trigger. First, you've got to get your guns and gear to a spot where the shooting is good, which involves navigation and seamanship, about which we, fortunately, didn't have to worry much. Then there are such things to know as the basic principles of jacket guns and wire wound guns and radial expansion guns, and bag ammunition and case ammunition and black powder and smokeless powder and centrifugal plungers and azimuth heads and firing charges and booster charges. There is the roll and pitch of the ship to consider, your speed and course and the target speed and course, deflection, air density, temperature of powder, vertical parallax and horizontal parallax, and trunnion tilt, and flarebacks and backfires. There are vector lines and local control and director fire and speed rings and blowbacks and range finders and range keepers and gas ejectors and various other ingredients of firing mechanism and the firing problem.

Those were things a naval gunnery officer on a big ship must know, but we, with our three-week mimeograph course, were happily ignorant of most of them. We found that for ordinary four-inch shooting you can get by in fair shape by using your eyes and being able to do simple arithmetic.

We got the range by taking a good look and shooting. Our spotter, high up in the crow's-nest, phoned the results, up 200 or down 200, depending on whether we were long or short, and we corrected our range. It was as simple as that.

All shots and ranges were recorded, both through the peep sight at the gun and by range finders from the bridge control station. I fired ten rounds watching two guns; on one we got three hits, on the other, two. That was pretty good shooting and I was mighty proud of the crews.

Our third day we got some antiaircraft practice against a target towed by a plane. I have always been glad the pilot didn't know what kind of experience lay behind those bursts that kept closing in about him. Maybe he guessed. But anyhow, we had learned enough from our mimeograph sheets about judging altitude and bearings and leading the target so that we turned in a fairly good shooting score. We came back from the week-end cruise feeling like old salts. The officers—Lieutenant Commander Jacoby, the skipper; Lieutenant Powell, executive officer; and Lieutenant Dan Johnson, gunnery officer—had done their best to make seagoing fighting men of us in the few brief days we could be with them. They toiled far into the night to make sure that we were given an opportunity to learn everything we would have to know. We were just one small part of an endless line of men being rushed through their capable hands, but they gave to us of their time as if we were the only gunnery pupils left in the world. I have never ceased being grateful for those precious training-ship days.

Back at school we paraded about like veterans. We had been to sea, we had fired genuine projectiles, and we thought we were ready for actual combat duty. The Navy had the same idea. Three weeks after we had started training at the Creek, our orders came through. We all had billets and we were all going to sea.

All but one—Berry. My schoolmastering in civilian life had undone me. I was to remain at the school as an instructor. The commanding officer had decided it was necessary to increase his staff and I was it. Commander Vail needed instructors, I knew that, and there was never a better officer to serve under. But I had tasted naval life for three beautiful days afloat and I was sick with disappointment. I remembered what Lieutenant Commander Jacoby had said to me aboard the training ship: "You are always a teacher in the Navy. If your men can't do the job properly it's because you haven't taught them correctly." That thought cheered me somewhat. But then the teaching plan somehow broke down, and a week later I got orders to report for sea duty. I fled from the Creek before any Navy minds could entertain a different idea, and joined my training companions, who were still waiting for their ships to get guns. Together we learned that our billets were finally ready in various ports. It looked as if, maybe, we were going to sea.

6

Our seagoing prospect filled all of us with greatest excitement. The few brief weeks at the Creek had effectively conditioned us for what might lie ahead. It is really quite amazing, the speed with which the Navy can divest a man of his civilian ways and notions and cultivate in him a zest for adventure and battle. We were not assailed by fears or regrets as we prepared to take final leave of our wives and families. We were genuinely eager to get going. The job before us seemed enormously important and we took pride in the fact that we were among those who were going out to "hold the line."

For we were in glorious company. It was the time when the fields of Bataan were bloody, the East Indies were falling, Russia was bending before the Nazi hordes, and those valiant few of Churchill's England were binding their wounds and springing again to an unequal fight. It was the time when the Battle of the Atlantic was half lost and pressing close to our shores, and U-boats skulked in the very heart of our harbors.

We knew that we, like the others already in the struggle, were going out with inadequate training and equipment, but we knew the reason why. The line had to be held. There was no time then for falling back. The harried few of our people who had learned the arts of war were faced with almost insurmountable problems of production and personnel, and there was no choice but to send men out to fight poorly armed and insufficiently trained.

The war was going badly, but, to tell the truth, the ten of us from the Creek were too concerned with our personal preparations for it to be much worried about the broader action. We fretted at reports of guns not ready, of gear not to be had, of ammunition that could not be allocated to merchant ships because it was needed elsewhere, of the too-few ships still not under way because the cargoes for their yawning bellies were bottlenecked in some distant plant.

But we knew too that the fighting spirit of the nation was up. We knew that holding the line would have meaning, for it would bring the enormous weight and brawn of 130 millions into the struggle. Those few short, hectic weeks at the Creek had schooled us firmly in the fighting traditions of the country and the Navy. Our assignment looked good to us, and we were anxious to get at it, trained and equipped or not.

We were as ignorant as any men who ever set out to sail the seas, and yet there was not a great deal that anyone could have taught us. Just what our problems might be, no one knew exactly. We had heard in the classroom about British and Canadian experience, and benefited from that, but, at the moment, it was generally agreed that what had been done against submarines in the past wasn't quite enough. The new techniques, the right answers, we would have to discover for ourselves and God help us if we failed. We would know what to do when the time for action came, provided our guns would shoot far enough and fast enough —the drills took care of that—but the problems of darkened ship, effective watches, of communication within the convoy, of general co-ordination of antisubmarine effort, and of relations with the civilian crews, who at the time were not convinced that the Armed Guard was God's gift to the Merchant Marine, were something we would have to work out through grim experience.

Neither problems nor subs, our reason for being, really worried us much those first days out of school. War then had its glamorous side, the sea its endless appeal. And we were going to sea! Most of us were hopeless landsmen, lawyers, salesmen, teachers and office workers who, save for the training cruise, had been no closer to the ocean than a week end at the beach or an evening with Conrad, or Melville, or Tomlinson. The prospect of tramping the decks, of visiting strange ports, of answering the call to battle stations utterly beguiled us. I guess I was the worst of the lot. I was too excited to think or eat. I hated to leave Anne, but that decision had been made when I joined up, and she, like a sailor's good wife, shared all my enthusiasm for the adventure ahead.

If we had scurried before, getting together uniforms and gear for the period of training, it was as nothing. Now I needed everything. I didn't know where we were going, but we expected to be away a long time. Consequently I immediately engaged on the one great shopping expedition of my life. Normally I dislike to buy things, probably because of my years on the other side of the counter. But Anne, who had superintended the original uniform purchases, entered into this new phase of my naval career with zest, and in a few hours we had the house jammed with equipment.

It was ridiculous, of course, for I knew well enough that in the barracks at school we had room only for collars, ties and socks and if we tried to bring anything else aboard it was promptly relegated to zero deck. But I didn't know where we were going and somehow I got a notion that the Merchant Marine was a little more commodious and comfortable than barracks quarters. It was my first big mistake, not only because I showed a childish indifference to the possibility of being torpedoed, but because a bunk on a merchant vessel is scarcely big enough to breathe in, and your stowage space is limited to the area beneath it. But anyhow, both Anne and I had a lot of fun in the ships' service stores, and every item of purchase delighted me.

I knew there was a good chance that we might go north, and so we bought heavily of sweaters, jackets, woolen underwear and socks. Also the possibilities were equally good that we would go south, so a sun helmet, goggles, whites, and light gear were in order. In addition there were considerable miscellaneous impedimenta I seemed to require, in addition to Navy issue. And a friend had given me a fine fishing kit that had to be included. My electric razor I could never use, for it might broadcast a trail to the subs, nor my camera, for photographs were strictly forbidden, but somehow I couldn't bring myself to part with either of them. Consequently I did a splendid job of equipping myself to the end that I should lose the finest wardrobe and collection of accessories I ever possessed the first time we were torpedoed. I went to sea like an ancient Viking, with all my worldly goods about me. After that I knew better.

The night before I was to entrain for the port city both Anne and I were far too excited to sleep. When we finally did retire, it seemed that I leaped from bed every half hour to add something new to the collection of gear. The stack completely obscured my sea chest, but I was determined to have everything along.

In the morning Anne and I said good-by. We thought it best that she should not go down to our entraining point, for neither of us by then was too steady emotionally and I had no desire to arouse the sympathies of my brother officers. So I dragged my supplies into a waiting cab, kissed Anne a last farewell, and was off, so I thought.

Our train was supposed to leave at nine o'clock, but at eleven we were still stomping around in the dust and at 11:30 it was announced that we wouldn't leave until 1500—3:00 P.M. This was a clear command from fate. I called

Anne. My excuse was that I had forgotten something, and
I casually suggested that we might as well have lunch together.

We parted again at one o'clock, Anne being very staunch
about it all, and at three o'clock it was announced that our
train would not depart until seven. For about thirty minutes I thought it over. All my instincts told me that no
woman can say good-by to a man three times in a single day.
I had visions of Anne actually shooing me out of the house.
But I couldn't waste three and a half precious hours. So I
called again, feeling a little as Lazarus must have felt when
he stalked from the grave: it was a terrific anticlimax.

The third call did it. We had determined to be conserva-
tive and sensible. We had stoically decided that of course I
would be back soon and no special obsequies on our parting
would be proper. But, as I have said, three good-bys are at
least one too many. That night when we left at nine o'clock,
Anne was aboard the train with me. We would have a day
in port before sailing, and we intended to make the most of
it.

On the train, Anne and I had opportunity to think of
what was really ahead. It would be months, perhaps, before
we would be together again. She was pregnant, and intended to take a position until it was time for the baby. She
was so apparently unworried about the prospects that she
put me completely at ease. I didn't know then, of course,
that I would be away at the time she needed me most, but I

think we both were somewhat aware of the possibility and simply elected not to face it.

We had fun seeing the town that last night. The country was pretty excited about things then, and I discovered that there were countless amiable citizens around the night clubs who were only too happy to entertain a man in uniform and his girl friend, provided we would listen just a little to their experiences in World War I, or to the reasons why they hadn't gone into service this time. But they were really very nice, and they made our evening of night clubs something we could never possibly have experienced without their kindnesses.

We kept up our celebration far beyond the time the doctor would have advised, but, since Anne was drinking only straight water, and partook lightly of food, we were sure Junior wouldn't mind. That night was something special. The schoolmaster was going to sea. He looked mighty fine in his uniform, so we both thought, and Anne was never prettier. The war, right at that moment, seemed particularly glamorous, and all the hard, solid training and talk they had given us in school vanished into nothingness.

Early the next day I said a final good-by to Anne and went down to the Center to meet the members of my crew. I had thought that I was excited until I saw them. I was prepared to make a great show of calmness, but it wasn't necessary. The men were in no state to observe how their officer was behaving. They were thinking only of our ship.

Was she there in the harbor? Which one was she? How big are the guns? Don't forget to salute the ensign! Where's Lefty?—he was stiff last night. Avast there, dammit, that's my gear! How soon will we see a sub? Just where in hell are we going anyway?

7

I went to the Port Director's office where I picked up identification charts, ordnance pamphlets on the guns we would use, and the first copy of Navy Regulations I had ever seen. Also they pushed into my hands the Armed Guard Bible—official title, *Instructions for the Commanding Officers of Naval Armed Guard Crews Aboard Merchant Ships in Time of War.*

Thus equipped I started down to the ship, which was sitting in the yards being armed and otherwise refitted. The *Scotty* * was really a beauty, as merchant ships go. She bulged amidships like a Hottentot and she had a poop like the *Santa Maria,* but, riding high in the water, she was steady as a cake of soap in a bathtub, and I had a hunch, come hell or high water, the *Scotty* would take it. She had been in the coastwise trade for years, her decks were greasy with the ore that had crossed them, and the paint had not been scraped for months. But the *Scotty* was a good 490 feet from stem to stern, and she could put 12,000 tons into her holds, and to me that was a ship! I was proud to make her acquaintance.

My boys had gone on ahead of me, and as I came up the ladder they were there to meet me. They were wildly en-

---

* The real name of the ship is not divulged for reasons of security.

thusiastic about what they had found aboard, but Goodwin, a husky lad from South Carolina, was the only one who could get his words out.

"Mistuh Berry!" he said. "Boy, is this sumpin'! We got a special table, a special waiter, an' we're gonna orduh aoh meals from a menu! Boy, we kin even pick out what we wanna eat!"

I knew then the trip would be a success. You can put a sailor under fire, you can send him into a mine field, you can set him adrift on the Pacific and you'll hear no complaint as long as the food situation is taken care of. It looked as if we and the *Scotty* were friends.

As I stepped to the deck I promptly wondered how the gun crew could be so happily preoccupied with thoughts of dinner and so oblivious to the pandemonium about them. Everything aboard was absolute confusion. The *Scotty* had been built in 1919, and she was in now for a complete refitting after a trip to Africa. It seemed that all the work had been left to the last day. Welders, carpenters, metal workers, stevedores and gunsmiths, comprising a veritable horde of ship fitters, were running madly about, stopping to apply a wrench here, a hammer there, and to give everything a quick once-over with a blow torch. Cranes were swinging bags of cargo aboard, gun shields were being riveted into position across the decks, a huge gun dangled over the aftergun platform as a squad of workmen attempted to swing it into place. Electric cables, hose lines, fuel lines, and torch feed lines ran everywhere, whipping across the decks like huge snakes as the workmen yanked them into position. It didn't seem that we could sail for weeks. I had visions of taking to the streets in an attempt to find quarters for the men and I wondered how Goodwin would like the automat.

The captain and his officers were ashore, but I finally found the purser, who did not seem interested in having passengers aboard, even if they were supposed to keep the *Scotty* clear of subs. The purser seemed to feel that putting guns on a merchant ship was asking for trouble. Still, he became affable enough when it appeared certain that he would have us whether or not he liked it and he showed us to the quarters for the men. My own cabin wasn't ready, and I would have to stay ashore until it was prepared.

The men grabbed their sea bags and went aft with me. Their quarters were really very good—a large recreation room toward the after part of the ship. It was at least fifteen by twenty feet in size, and fourteen bunks had been installed. We immediately tore out four of them and hid them so they couldn't put anyone else in with us.

I divided the crew into two watch sections and posted the men, for the time, on a four-hour watch schedule. Then I went with my coxun to inspect the guns. None of them had been installed, so we started back to quarters, deviating a little to look over the ship.

She was filthy dirty. No one had attempted to clean up after the cargo of raw ore, and the new crew had not been

TRAINING SHIP

The hot shellman (wearing asbestos gloves, lower right) is preparing to catch an ejected shell casing after the gun has been fired.

Official U. S. Navy Photograph

ACK-ACK
The Armed Guard crew works out on an antiaircraft gun.

signed. Not that that made any difference. She never was cleaned up. We decided to look at the mess hall, to see if Goodwin's dream might be true. There was a pile of garbage on the deck just aft of the mess, and it was beginning to crawl. I poked my head into the galley. There stood the cook with a cleaver, looking wild-eyed at two big cockroaches who were fighting each other to see which would get first crack at the cook. I pulled back and led Coxun Ritter away—I knew that he leaned to the squeamish side. The passageways were full of rubbish and litter and we went on deck again for a breath of air. The crowd of workmen had cleared somewhat and by this time I was in a soberer mood and able to look at our ship a little objectively. The decks were caked with rust and most of the gear was rusty and tossed all over the decks and this, combined with the air lines, fire lines, cables for deck lights and cargo lights, made me feel again that I had stepped into a junk yard full of serpents. I looked at Ritter, and Ritter looked sad. I decided that the only thing to do was put the men to work. They had survived the first glimpse of the ship through their enthusiasm at getting to sea, but I knew it couldn't last long unless all hands were busy. So I ordered the entire crew to turn to in their quarters—those could be clean at any rate—and I went forward for a look at my cabin, which was next the captain's, directly below the bridge.

Compared to the decks and passageways, the cabin was clean. It had a built-in bunk with drawers underneath, a closet, a wash basin, mirror, water bottle, and swinging desk top. The room was so small that I would have to go outside into the passageway to put on my pants, but it looked as if it had been cleaned at some time or other and it had cross ventilation and a good big fan. I felt lucky and I returned in better humor to see how the men were faring.

They had turned to with a will, and immediately demonstrated the ability of a sailor to make a home in a cracker box. Pictures of girl friends were scotch-taped to the bulkheads, calendars covered up damaged corners, the swab and squilgee had been broken out and the deck glistened. The men were crowded, but they were happy, and Ritter had refrained from speaking of the garbage pile near the mess hall.

The work went on well without me, so I ventured back through the ship again. I wanted to get to know her before the officers and crew came aboard. I was a little awed by the size of her; I had never seen one that big before. I wasn't scared—I didn't know enough to be scared. I was somewhat bewildered by the whole thing and I wondered just why in the devil I had decided on the Navy.

I went up on the bridge to think it over. So this was the Armed Guard. We would float around on this damned garbage scow, afraid we wouldn't sight a sub, and scared that we would. Our job was to keep the submarines below the surface and the raiders away. We would be commended, even if our ship sunk and we never got a shot, provided the sub didn't surface. But even though we saved the ship, if the sub surfaced and we didn't get a shot at him, we could expect to be censured. That means if you take a torpedo and all hell breaks loose below decks you stay there with the guns and make sure that sub doesn't surface until you get a crack at him. Sometimes you get one. Other times you have to wait a little too long and the water wets your feet up on the gun deck and then it's a bit late.

I could hear one of our instructors speaking: "You aren't supposed to attack, only to defend. That's the hard part of the job. Other fellows get to go out and take a crack at them, but you're supposed to be pleased when an alarm turns out to be false. You can't go hunt for them. If you hear a sub or a raider you're supposed to run away and fight only if necessary. That gets on your nerves—the constant alert, the constant strain. You wish you could see something, or go after something, but you can't. . . ."

Berry had it out with himself, that afternoon on the bridge of the *Scotty*. I thought of the men below, wisecracking and hanging pictures. I was disgusted with myself. A hell of an officer I was. I stood up and mentally kicked myself in the pants. That was the end of that sort of thing. We had a job to do, and right at the moment it was a pretty tough job and pitying yourself wouldn't help it any. I took another look around. I stood up on the bridge and puffed out my chest and decided the *Scotty* was a pretty big ship and those guns would be pretty big guns and if we got one good shot, just one, we could call everything even. I crossed my fingers and hoped everything would come out all right.

Then I went below and put half the crew on liberty and went out to look for a room.

8

My crew members were all Southerners, save for Ritter the coxun, who came from Ohio. Ritter had served a hitch in the Navy before, leaving in 1928 to become a policeman. He was called back and given a coxswain's rating when the war started. Most of the other boys had never been to sea before. They were mainly lads of eighteen and nineteen and only two of them had gone to high school. Jordan, from West Virginia, had been in the Army. How he managed the transfer to the Navy he never explained. His father was a minister, Jehovah's Witnesses, Jordan said, and the boy himself was very religious. He read his Bible every day, and he was a good crew member. He was the only one aboard who seemed to know what orders meant, in the beginning. His fine discipline was a big help to me. He was my sight setter, and every morning he reported that he dreamed the night before that he had got a sub. I have a great fondness for Bible-reading sailors. They make good fighting men.

One of the boys had been a steel worker in the Florida shipyards. He was earning eighty dollars a week and when his draft number came up he enlisted in the Navy. He was my problem child. Somehow, he blamed the Navy for his loss of income, and he particularly resented me. He hated to take orders. He was one of the few men in the Navy I have known who turned out to be a trouble maker. Another of the lads, Brown—we lost him the first time we were torpedoed—had been a railroad brakeman and was one of the finest men you could meet. Our signalman was from Oklahoma. He had made a trip into the Pacific on a Navy transport, and was our seagoing veteran. Johnson had come out of college to join the Navy. He had a dream—to write a book about the Armed Guard. I encouraged him in his desire, and several times he actually started it, but then we were sunk and he lost his notes and gave up in disgust. I wish Johnson had written his book; then this one wouldn't be necessary. I hope, wherever he is, he'll feel this has something in it he wanted to say. Johnson is a good man. When the war ends, if his luck holds, he'll be teaching English back in Oklahoma. I think I'd like his course in writing practice. Certainly Johnson will never lack for subjects to suggest to his students.

My best man was Harmon, who had been assistant manager of one of the Firestone distributing stations. Harmon had joined the Navy because he had long believed we ought to stop the Axis, and now that we were out to do that necessary job, Harmon felt his place was on the firing line. He was aggressive and reliable. He looked upon the guns as his personal possessions and would spend long hours caring for them, whether or not he had orders. The rest of the men couldn't understand Harmon. He would stand in the hot sun, bared to the waist, dreaming happily as he applied the grease swab or chipped the paint. The five-incher meant something special to Harmon. He told me once that he had talked about getting into the war, and now he was doing something about it, and that made him happy. I never knew another man to have quite the same sense of righteousness about what he was doing. The rest of us simply knew that our cause is most just and that we had to do our damnedest. With Harmon, fighting the war was a kind of religion. He was the oldest man in the crew, but the first to reach a gun when Battle Stations sounded, the last to leave when all hands were ordered to abandon ship.

The fair-haired lad of our outfit was Gallegos. It was Gallegos who started the singing; it was Gallegos who organized the jam sessions with his harmonica; it was Gallegos who knew the best stories, who won at poker, who was the first choice of the girls in port. Gallegos was absolutely indifferent to the war, to Navy Regulations, or to any task immediately before him. He could grin his way out of more work than any other man I ever saw. He was lean and long and sandy-haired, and his white teeth flashing in his tanned face gladdened your heart whenever you saw him. Gallegos was lazy and unreliable and he could have the ship any time he wanted it. He had played football down in Florida and he used to come up to the bridge and sit with me and we'd talk football by the hour.

Altogether we had nine men and the coxun in the crew. I can't honestly say that any of them liked the Navy at first, except Harmon. The life was too new to them, they had been rushed around too much, and they were homesick.

9

The second day I went back aboard the *Scotty* and set up
a station bill in order to get as much work done as possible
before sailing. Our schedule called for morning chow at
7:30, all bunks to be made shipshape and quarters cleaned
and scrubbed down by 8:30. The period from 8:30 to 11:30
was for assigned duties: cleaning the guns, which were being rapidly put into place, cleaning the magazines, mount-
ing our tension racks for the 20-mm. guns, preparing stowage space for our supplies, and putting our gear in good
condition. From 1200 to 1300 (1:00 P.M.) we had noonday
chow and a rest period, and from 1300 to 1630 (4:30 P.M.)
we worked on the gun quarters. Until we sailed, half the
crew was to get liberty each day from 1630 until 0730 the
following morning, with half the crew standing four-hour
heel and toe watches on alternate days, that is, four hours on
and four hours off. We were required by Navy Regulations
to keep a watch on all guns of six pounds or over.

There seemed to be hundreds of ships in the yards being
armed and the procurement of supplies presented a genuine
problem. We practically had to forage for what we needed
and the biggest difficulty was, of course, that I was never
certain I knew exactly what we needed. Finally, after considerable chiseling and haggling and a bit of borrowing

from the ships' engineers about the yards, I managed to get together enough soap, oils, greases and tools to clean up the guns and get them into condition for possible action. When we finally did obtain some supplies we had nowhere to stow them. We practically stole a storage room, a little cubicle that somehow had been missed in the cargo plan, and in it we constructed shelves and bins. There were no lights in this room, so I begged a flashlight from the Port Director, and with that we took care of our stowage problem.

Once we had conquered the problem of supplies we turned to the guns. The ship was still taking on cargo, and the ship fitters were as busy as ever, but at least some of the guns were in position and I decided that we had better become thoroughly familiar with them as soon as possible. We first turned to on the five-inch on the stern. So help me, I had never seen a five-inch gun before in my life. However, as they frequently told us at school, the basic principle of all guns is that you put a projectile in one end and it comes out the other, so we didn't hesitate to go to work on her.

It was then I discovered that the ready boxes for the gun were put on backward. These boxes contain the ammunition for emergency purposes, until the regular ammunition hoist can get into operation, so of course the boxes are supposed to be as convenient as possible. Split seconds count when Battle Stations sounds, and no one wants to lose any time.

I went to the foreman of the welders and told him about

ATLANTIC

the ready boxes. He wasn't impressed. Backward or forward, it was all the same to him. I ranted and stormed, but still no results. The ready boxes had been welded on the deck, and there they were going to stay. There was nothing anyone could do about it.

If we couldn't change the ship we would have to change our technique. In my crew was a good, husky left-hander from Virginia. He could load the heavy projectile from the wrong side of the gun. That solved our problem. The procedure was against Navy policy but it was the only way we could get any speed or system in our loading technique. As far as our welders were concerned, Navy policy be damned.

We had aboard, in addition to our five-inch gun, four batteries of 20-mm.'s. These last, known to the Navy as the "Sailor's Sweetheart," were really fine. The 20-mm. is an automatic machine gun which fires shells at a rate of 400 rounds per minute. The shells are held in a drum which feeds them into the firing chamber by means of a spring. An interesting feature of this gun is its removable barrel. When the barrel in the gun becomes so hot that it slows up the firing, it can be removed, dunked into a pot of water to cool, and a new barrel inserted. Or, if no new barrel is available, a bucket of sea water can be dumped over the barrel in the gun and firing can be resumed without injury to it. In addition to our twenties we also had the usual .30-caliber guns, very handy gadgets for training purposes and for shooting sharks. This, of course, was the equipment we had at that

81

time on the *Scotty*. Present equipment is superior, and something we can't discuss.

As we lay in port, waiting for sailing orders, we had plenty of time to get the gun crews thoroughly organized and I assigned the men to their jobs. The major gun stations for surface fire vary somewhat with the size of the weapon, but in general are: the pointer, whose duty it is to lay the gun up or down and to do the actual firing of the piece under the local control system used by the Armed Guard; the trainer, who trains or moves the gun on a horizontal arc; and the sight-setter, who moves the pointers that set the range and scale which are passed to him by the fire-control officer.

When the gun is being trained and pointed for actual firing, the range and bearing of the target are obtained by the fire-control officer or a crew member placed near the highest point of the ship. A range finder, or director, or ordinary pelorus may be used. Once it is determined how the gun should be depressed or elevated in order to hit the target, this information is telephoned to the sight-setter. It is his job to set the mechanism of the gun so that it will be at proper elevation when it is on target. Meanwhile the pointer and trainer sit at their sights and crank away, making sure that the gun is kept "on target" in spite of the changes effected by the sight-setter. The gun must be "on target" at all times, despite the roll and pitch of the ship. That is all the men at the gun have to worry about, besides getting it loaded, locking the breech, and watching out for flarebacks and a few similar things. It is the fire-control officer who figures out the firing problem.

At actual Battle Stations the sight-setter wears a pair of headphones through which he receives all firing data and commands to the crew from the officer in charge—in this case me—who may be on the bridge or at some designated fire-control station. The gun captain, usually an enlisted man or a petty officer, supervises the loading of the guns. He sees that the shell is safely and securely seated in the chamber, closes the breech, and gives the orders: "Ready 1, ready 2, ready 3," to the shellmen. The third shellman obtains the shell from the ready box, passes it to the second shellman, who, part of a human chain, whips it on to the first shellman, who puts it into the chamber. When the shellmen respond to the "ready" order, and the pointer and trainer announce they are "on target" and the sight-setter has fixed the range and scale and calls "set," the order to fire is given. Then the hot shellman catches the expended cartridge and disposes of it by tossing it overboard, out of the way of the crew.

The procedure I have described is for case ammunition guns. The larger guns on big warships use bag ammunition. The case shell is the kind we are all familiar with, the projectile fitting into the case which contains the powder. Bag ammunition consists of a projectile and a silken bag of powder which is rammed into the gun. For our five-inch gun we had a trayman instead of a hot shellman. The trayman inserts a steel tray into the breech, which prevents the breech from burring when the projectile is inserted. When bag ammunition is used the gun captain has the additional duty of blowing the gun, clearing away the tiny traces of silk from the powder bag which otherwise might catch fire from the hot gun and explode the next bag of powder before the breech can be closed. Also, one of the shellmen acts as a rammerman—sounds like the spirit of '76. It is his duty to seat the projectile with a wooden rammer which he uses on the base of the projectile before the powder bag is inserted.

When a battle is on, the men of the gun crew work like mad and the noise and confusion is of course terrific. I had to order sand painted onto our gun decks to give the men decent footing. The gun captain shouts his orders and the men respond at the top of their voices. When the sight-setter has the correct range set he doesn't give an order at all, but instead deals the pointer a good, hefty whack on the posterior. The pointer then will fire the gun immediately when he has it "on target."

Submarines attack so abruptly that it was once impossible to use any range-finding equipment, even if you had it. We have relied on "spotting" to get our range, which is simply a trial-and-error method of getting hits. We put our first shot on the side of the submarine nearer our ship, and the second shot on the other side. Then, if the splashes are observed carefully, and the range estimated correctly, the third shot can be placed directly on the U-boat. That is the straddle method. There is also the ladder method, which means that you fire the first shot short of the sub and then change your deflection and increase the range until you get him. These methods are slow, and speed is always vital, but it would be impossible to get a hit without some consistent firing plan. Fortunately for us, American genius and the production of American factories have now made available to smaller ships the range-finding mechanisms given only to large ships of war when we first went to sea.

Spotting procedure, demanding a rapid firing of the guns, calls for considerable drill, but after four hours a day for three weeks ashore, and drill every day at sea, a crew can carry out the entire loading and firing schedule with such speed that, with the three-inch gun, average gunners can put out twelve to fifteen rounds a minute. The new guns are considerably faster.

Not all the men in the gun crews aboard merchant ships are Navy men. We attempt to man the pointer, trainer, sight-setter and gun captain with Navy men, and for the rest of the positions we train the merchant seamen while at sea. Incidentally, in more than a year and a half of working with merchant seamen crews, my experience has been that only one man has refused to serve at a gun station, although this additional duty does not bring extra pay. This one man, I discovered on questioning him, had previously been aboard a merchant ship where the gun-crew members had told him to get out of the way and let them do the work and he was probably justifiably insulted. On the whole the attitude of the merchant seamen toward serving on the guns has been fine, according to my experience. They have been willing, they have taken instruction without wanting overtime pay, and in many instances they have asked for more detailed instructions and have been of great assistance in repairing minor breakdowns of the guns.

We organized our crews and were ready for the war, except that, even after eight days, we had no ammunition. Baker, the red flag signifying that ammo is being loaded, had never once been hoisted. I grew worried. Were we going to sea or weren't we? I hadn't been able to supplement my crew with merchant seamen because a crew hadn't yet been signed. Here we were, eight days at sea and we were still warped tightly to the dock.

Finally, on the evening of the eighth day, a group of merchant sailors poured aboard. I say "poured" advisedly. But, drunk or sober, those men could handle a ship. The pilot came aboard, the engines rumbled, and the members of my crew sent up a shout when it finally was discovered that we were actually under weigh.

I was very proud of that crew as I stood on the bridge, near the pilot and mate, watching the lights of the town and the red and green navigation lights of the ships constantly swarming across the harbor. The boys had worked hard, and they had accomplished a lot. Working conditions were bad, and yet not a man had grumbled.

As I stood there, thrilling to the throb of the engines under the decks, drinking up salty night air and feeling, with a swell of exultation, that I was finally and actually a Navy man at sea, a sudden horrible thought struck me. We had gone off and left the captain.

I suppose it was the sight of the pilot boat, bearing down upon us with its red and white lights, that brought up from my subconscious those frantic thoughts about the missing captain. For the pilot boat signaled and came alongside, a ladder went over, there was a great stir on deck, the mate took the wheel, the pilot left the bridge and it became known to me, without anyone saying it, that the captain was aboard.

He stomped up to the bridge immediately without speaking a word to anyone. My first glimpse of him came as he stopped a moment in the faint light of the binnacle. He was squat and gray and grim, and he made me think immediately of those aging fishermen who sit mending their nets on a Sunday afternoon in the harbor at Gloucester. He quickly looked things over, gave me a bare glance, and then stomped out again.

I learned to love old Captain Olafson the few short days I had to know him. He was kindly and considerate in a severe, gruff manner that left you aware of his gentle humanity only upon later reflection. Captain Olafson had gone

to sea as a boy with the square-rigged ships and he remained
ever faithful to them. In his years at sea he had skippered
a good many modern freighters along many thousands of
miles of coast line, but, until now, he had not taken one of
the contraptions far to sea. It seemed he preferred to think
that only the ancient square-riggers, running bravely in the
wind, could really stand up against the might of the ocean
and he disliked to prove for himself that this was not true.
At any rate, I know he felt strongly against making this
trip, but the lure of a big bonus had been too much for him.
This, Captain Olafson frequently told me, was to be his last
time out. He would retire again, and for good, using his
bonus to complete the payments on his farm in upper New
York state. He had the usual sailor's sentiment for his own
plot of ground, an emotion quite false in them, but nevertheless fervently nurtured by most of the seafaring men I have
met.

10

We moved to a new port to take on our precious ammunition and more cargo. There we were thrown out of our stowage room because the steward's department needed it for supplies. That was our first intimation of the length of time we would be out, an augury that pointed to a long stretch at sea. We found new space for our supplies, in the lazarette, a space we could have because it was so dark, dirty, hot and small that no one else wanted it. We made it do, the men patiently rebuilding the shelves and bins by flashlight. We stowed our ammunition safely in the magazines, loaded our ready boxes, and again we felt that we were ready to go to sea.

But merchant ships sail when they bulge with cargo, not before. If the cargo isn't ready, they wait for it. Somewhere, in some factory, something had gone wrong. Our cargo, urgently needed at the front, wasn't ready, and once more we waited.

We wanted to make good use of our time and I decided that the delay would afford an excellent opportunity to work out the men on the five-inch gun. For that first drill I had no experience to guide me in naming the men to the stations. My crew had never worked on a five-inch gun;

like me, most of them had never before seen one. So I just pointed to men at random, saying, "You're the trainer, you're the pointer, you're the sight-setter." Then we conducted what was probably the lousiest gun drill in the world. We got the thing loaded and unloaded without its going off, but I didn't want to take a chance again. I had heard that there was a five-inch loading machine in the yard. I went ashore, found an old chief gunner's mate who agreed to become our instructor, loaded my crew into a truck and went over to the armory where we spent four hours in drill on loading the five-inch. When you know that the five-inch projectile weighs fifty pounds and the powder bags weigh twenty-five pounds each, you can appreciate the physical condition we were in when we finished. But we were loading the required ten rounds per minute.

After the experience with the five-inch gun, I decided to see what we could do with the 20-mm. All our previous practice, save for that on the training ship, had been more or less theoretical, even if we did go through the actual motions. It was not a particularly good spot for it, but I wanted to see if those "Sailor's Sweethearts" really would fire. Some of them would, enough to convince us, but others stayed mute. So we dragged out our ordnance pamphlets, looked at the pictures, took the guns down, and then put them together again. Then we resumed our tests. We continued this process, tinkering with the mechanism here and there according to our various individual notions of what was wrong, until finally, and miraculously, we had all the guns in firing condition. Then I sat down and wrote a letter to the Port Director telling him what I thought he ought to tell green new Armed Guard officers.

11

Finally, almost two weeks after we initially went aboard, we actually shoved off to sea. It was a great moment. The men were in highest spirits despite the long tussle with the five-inch loading machine the day before, and the members of the merchant crew threw off their early lethargy and went purposefully about their business. This, we guessed, was it. The engines moaned, the propellers throbbed, the *Scotty,* laden down to the water line, rolled gracefully, like a bibulous but dignified lady, and we put away from shore with a determination that indicated someone, at least, knew where he was going.

I was watching from the bridge. The pilot finished his chores, took his departure, and Captain Olafson took over. I felt a great confidence in him. He was old—I couldn't guess how old—but he stood there stanch as oak, his clear eyes scanning the breakers, his weather-worn face strong and expectant, as if he could hardly wait to sniff the genuine salt air, untainted by touch of earth.

We had not gone far when the mess boy brought a radio message from Sparks. The skipper read it, grunted, gave the wheel to the mate after ordering a course that caused the mate to throw him a quick questioning look. Captain Olafson did not respond to the look. He went to his cabin and for the next two hours I was too engrossed in the seascape to think about him.

Then suddenly Captain Olafson appeared on deck, dressed like a retired farmer in his Sunday clothes—stiff collar, derby hat, and shiny black trousers that assumed the shape of his legs. He beckoned to me.

"Convoy conference," said the captain. "You'd better come along."

We made a port which I quickly recognized, and put to shore. The conference was short and to the point, although it omitted many details as to where we were going. At any rate it was made clear to us that the poor old *Scotty,* already heavily burdened, was to pick up still additional cargo before we actually put to sea. I don't think Captain Olafson was pleased, but he said nothing.

Outside, as we walked across the grounds, I saw a girl who looked mighty familiar to me. It didn't make sense, but I was certain she was Anne.

Even as I was deliberating on that impossibility, I heard her call: "Bob!"

By sheerest luck, Anne had come down to see a friend of mine about certain legal papers I had neglected to make out properly before leaving home. She had been unable to find him immediately, and consequently was delayed just long enough for us to see each other again. We had so many things to say we were scarcely able to talk at all.

I had completely forgotten about Captain Olafson. He

stepped aside discreetly, and finally I remembered him and presented him to Anne.

He made a sweeping bow, took her hand and addressed her in a courtly manner you rarely hear these days, except perhaps in the Deep South. Anne was charmed and fascinated, and when Captain Olafson told her not to worry and promised to take care of me personally, her eyes were brimming with tears. He was a grand old man, our captain. Anne and I will never forget him.

Sailing orders cut short this fourth and sweetest farewell, and we quickly made our way to sea again. A swarm of Inshore Patrol boats came out to guard us, and soon a big, silver blimp roared overhead, and now and then a civilian aircraft patrol plane would zoop by us. Shortly we saw that we were part of a convoy, an amazing long line of ships that seemed to cover the whole ocean. Vessels stretched for miles, each carefully keeping her station or suffering the humiliation of being herded into line by one of the swift-darting destroyers. The experience delighted me, and I couldn't pry myself from the bridge. I camped there until midnight, and then reluctantly went below, too excited to sleep.

Early the next day we ran into a heavy fog. It rolled in from seaward, great ragged swirls of mist that finally became so thick you couldn't see the bow from the bridge. Just as I came on deck the foghorn blasted and I almost fell down the hatchway. It sounded like a giant trumpet heralding the end of the world, and I had a momentary feeling that when we plowed through the next strip of muck we might very well slide off the sea and into some unfathomable abyss. Then, as I proceeded forward, the horn sounded again, and again I jumped, but finally, after having the experience repeated every sixty seconds, I began to grow accustomed to it.

Down the line of the convoy, other horns answered us. It was eerie, as if a herd of enormous cattle had been put to pasture among the clouds. I had posted a double watch and made my way around the deck to check the various stations. The sea had roughened during the night and I had difficulty adjusting my legs to the roll and pitch of the ship. I felt a little ill, but fortunately did not get actually seasick. As I approached the stern I saw two members of the merchant crew paying out a sea pig, or towing buoy, on a cable. The buoy looked something like a stovepipe and elbow thrust through a small wooden platform. The platform floated in the water, with the elbow submerged, open end forward. This caused the sea pig to spout a small column of water through the pipe which thrust up vertically from the platform. The idea was that the sea pig would be let out to a point where the ship following us could observe the water spout and keep clear.

We pushed steadily ahead at standard speed, sailing by our horn, one blast indicating that we were directing our course to starboard, two to port. During a brief lift in the fog I saw a destroyer gallop by, her sea pig setting up a spout of water. I was fascinated by this device, which so simply and effectively permitted a ship to mark her position.

The fog quickly closed in again, and the destroyer disappeared. Once more we were alone, driving through the wall of cloud, with the moan of the horns constantly tearing at our eardrums. I began to get worried. My crew members were at their watch stations, but it seemed we ought to be ready for battle drill. Anything might happen. I expected to see a submarine at any moment. Still, I knew we were inside the limits and that the only danger we might reasonably expect was from collision. That danger was much graver than I realized then. I was almost disappointed when the fog lifted and we could see the stars.

We sighted several wrecks then, their superstructure jutting out of the water, and I guessed that we were finally in the lane that so recently had been full of trouble for Allied merchant shipping. Once I jumped and my heart was in my mouth when I saw a black object break the water. After I got both feet back on deck again and looked at the object through my glasses, I perceived that it was a porpoise playing along beside the ship. I remember swallowing my heart and giving a sickly grin to the captain and saying to myself "Whoo!" It was about the only word I had spoken on my first watch at sea.

My dead reckoning was bad at the time, and I had no idea where we were, except I was sure we were far out in the Atlantic. I went below for coffee, and when I returned to the bridge we had come about and were heading into some kind of harbor. Again a pilot boat chugged out, there was a rattle of gear and a stir on deck, and the pilot came aboard. He promptly announced that it was too foggy to go in and he went to bed.

I attempted to follow his example, but by 1:00 A.M. I gave up. I was too excited to sleep. I went outside and prowled the decks. The fog was swirling in again. The ship was very big and very dark and lonely, and the foghorns kept a mournful din all about the harbor. The raw air soon chilled me through and I went below for coffee. There I stayed, shooting the breeze with the assistant engineer and the men from the off watch until morning. They told me the port we were making, and passed on scuttlebutt * to the effect we were bound for Persia, once we shoved off for keeps. That really finished off any ideas I might have had about sleeping.

At six o'clock the ship began stirring again. The mate shouted orders, the winches ground against the anchor chain, the pilot took his place near the wheel, the propellers furiously churned up water, and we pushed slowly into the fog and up to the pier. I watched fascinated as the seamen snared one of their lines on a bitt ashore, the cables ran out, and the ship drew snugly into her berth while the crisscross

---

* In sailing days a drinking fountain, around which sailors exchanged gossip. Thus, in the Navy, gossip and rumor are also termed "scuttlebutt."

of springers were secured to fix her in position. My crew awakened and came on deck, wide-eyed to find themselves in the heart of a city, when they had expected to be miles at sea. I arranged for a liberty party and took off to see the Port Director for additional supplies. There were none to be had. All I could dig up was a two-by-four to make a rammer for the big gun, and a gun tub.

12

We put the last of our cargo aboard, and we knew then beyond all peradventure of doubt that we were going to the wars. Big cranes walked over, extra planking was laid on the decks, and soon a little train of tanks rolled down to the wharf, chugging and rattling indignantly as if putting to sea was some kind of outrage against them. They were quickly secured into giant slings, and swung over our side as easily as a man might toss a sea bag over his shoulder. Then they dropped gently into place about the deck, properly distributed so they would not affect the stability of the ship, and the crew lashed them into place and secured them with huge timber blocks. The tanks, calked with tar and shrouded with tarpaulins after the work of securing them had been completed, looking like so many sleeping elephants. I had a feeling that any submarine commander viewing them through his periscope would know only too well what they were.

If I had any fears that the tanks on deck might attract a torpedo, they were promptly increased by our next item of cargo—airplanes for the European front. These were distributed among the tanks, lashed down, and secured with blocks. There was little room left. We were loaded with cargo to the overhead of the boat deck, and I felt sure that the scuttlebutt I had heard the night before was not far wrong.

The sight of that cargo set my nerves on edge. I was not frightened, but I had a full sense of our grave responsibilities as Armed Guards. It was our job to see that the precious planes and tanks, not to mention the assorted varieties of TNT stowed below, got to the intended destination. We would have to run a gantlet of submarines and enemy aircraft to do it, no matter where we were going. The odds were entirely against us. The rate of sinkings at the time was terrific. But we had our job to do. We couldn't let the subs surface, we couldn't permit a hostile plane to approach. That meant an alert, endless watch and quick and perfect action on the guns. I was determined that we would not fail through any fault of our own. I knew that the men would give everything they had.

I set up a permanent watch bill and a schedule of gun drills that probably would have evoked cries of horror from all of us back at school. But I knew that we couldn't stop submarines unless we saw them first, and the tip of a periscope, which looks something like a bit of gas pipe jutting from the water, is mighty difficult to see on a turbulent ocean.

The men on watch duty served four hours on deck, four hours off. When we ran into real danger areas, the time at watch was decreased to two hours, and when a warning

"FOLLOW TRACERS AND FIRE WHEN READY!"

The fire-control man, frequently the officer in charge, gives the order that means the end of an enemy plane.

SUNSET ON THE PACIFIC

Official U. S. Navy Photograph

of submarines was received, we used a double watch in twenty-minute shifts.

It is difficult to convey the anxiety and strain and loss of energy that goes with a watch at sea, particularly at night. Each man on duty was given a sector to sweep with his glasses. The sectors overlapped, so that there could be no blind spots in our scrutiny of the waves. The glasses weren't used at all times. It would prove practically impossible for a man to hold binoculars in position for hours on end, or to keep vigilant unless he could get relief by resorting to ordinary eyesight. However, we learned to employ little helps—a swivel frame to hold the glasses, or simply a crotched stick of wood, one end resting against the chest, the other supporting the glasses in position.

Still, the men take a beating when they're out on deck, in cold, raw night air, constantly on the alert for anything suspicious in the slightest degree. The least bit of flotsam, the sight of a fish playing in the water, the repeated sensation of sighting an object that always arises from tenseness and strain, any one of these common incidents of the average watch turns you cold with fear. It is not a fear of the possible sub, nor of what may happen if it really is a sub, but a terror born of your own desire to do the job right, to protect adequately the lives and property in your keeping.

We had a bad time with the watches those first days and nights. I say "we" for I seemed totally unable to sleep, and by night I was constantly on deck or on the bridge, scanning the waters and fearing the worst. Those first hours confirmed in me a habit I have never been able to lose at sea. I can't get rest at night. I must be up prowling, or leveling my glasses, checking the guns, inspecting the watches, making sure just once again that our communications are in order. I am sure that I'm not alone in that habit. Armed Guard officers, so far as I have been able to learn, are uniformly nocturnal animals. The night is too dangerous, and there is too much at stake for a comfortable rest when the sun is down. I have always trusted my men completely. I know that the watch, wherever he may be stationed, and whatever the hour, rubs his eyeballs out against the endless waves and that he never for an instant forgets his duty. I know that the crew will respond to Battle Stations in a split second, whether or not I am there. But still I can't shut my eyes when we're running the sub lanes at night.

The watch was only a small part of our task. We had to be ready for the Nazis when and if they appeared, and we felt pretty certain they would appear, some time or other. So we drilled. We were at the guns morning, afternoon and night, until darkness stopped us. It was vital that we perfect our keymen in their jobs, and it was necessary too that the merchant sailors be trained in their part of the work. There is no way to learn a gun properly outside hard, wearying drill. And, in a convoy, there can be no targets to fire at to make it fun. But not a man squawked. We learned those guns until they became a part of us.

13

There was a little fun aboard, despite the watches and drills and the cleaning and painting of guns that began as soon as we left harbor. Gallegos had a harmonica. The sounds he produced were not exactly music, but he could create a rhythmic wailing *um-pah* that the crew agreed was boogie-woogie and they listened entranced among the planes and tanks beside the fo'c'sle whenever Gallegos elected to entertain them.

And we were beginning to get acquainted. During the rest periods, when tension eased, we sat around talking about what we would do when the war ended. Somehow we never talked about the war. Most of us had done plenty of that before we actually got into it, but now there seemed to be no need for further belligerent conversation. We were in it, and that was that. Because of radio silence, we had no opportunity to obtain fresh news, but that didn't bother us. No one read anything but sports and the comic strips in the papers we had along. It was the magazines, and, among the men, the Western story magazines, that got the play. We were bound, we didn't know where, but unquestionably to high adventure and still our gunners got their thrills vicariously reading of the Wild West.

Most of the time we kept our station in the convoy, but

sometimes our enfeebled engines let us down, and we lost position. These mishaps didn't worry the captain a bit. Keeping station he held to himself, and was almost surly. The moment we were sailing independently, he blossomed forth in excellent humor and seemed to enjoy his trip. It was on such occasions that I sat with him on the bridge, listening to his stories of the sea, and hearing of his plans for the little farm in upper New York. Captain Olafson was a good friend. He did everything he could for the Navy crew and helped to make bearable our first precarious days aboard.

I am sorry I cannot say as much for the merchant crew. I have met fine merchant sailors aboard the *Scotty,* and I have met a great many of them since. I owe my life to one of them, DuQuoin, the little bandy-legged first assistant engineer on the *Scotty* who hailed from New Orleans and detested water, but who nevertheless took his chances with it to fish me out of the ocean after our first torpedoing. But far too great a number on that first voyage were not the cruise companions I would have deliberately chosen, and I know they felt the same way about Navy men, only more so.

I don't know yet just what there was about us that irked them. Perhaps it was merely that we were new to the ways of the sea, or that they felt we had usurped a job they could do themselves. At any rate many of them sneered at us as "ninety-day wonders" (they gave us a sixty-day break at that) and they goaded the men in the Navy crew about working for low Navy pay.

I was forced to tell the men that they should not permit themselves to be baited. But it was hard for them to hold their tempers. I remember a conversation between one of the Navy men—Shadd, I think—and a burly member of the black gang whose name I never learned.

"Listen, sucker," he was saying to our gunner, "you guys are the world's prize saps. You git in th' war to wear a uniform an' then you don't git a uniform. You think you're a gunner. Hell, what chance have you got to hit a sub? You'll be there tryin' for a shot when this damn scow sinks an' you'll never git one. An' if we don't git hit, what happens? You ride around in some goddam tub an' take orders an' you git into port without dough an' th' girls don't give you a play. You don't git no money. What th' hell do gunners git out of it anyway?"

Knowing Shadd, I figured he was going to get himself six feet of black gang right then and there. But he held his temper beautifully. He grinned at his challenger.

"Why," said Shadd, "gunners get glory." He grinned again.

"Glory!" snorted the seaman. "For Christ sake! Where can you spend it? What can you buy with it? What kind of bonus is that? . . . A little pink an' blue ribbon. . . ."

Shadd's grin disappeared and his jaw set. "Listen, you son-of-a-bitch," he said very calmly. "I'm in this because my country's in it and I'm damn proud to be in the United States Navy. Now, if you so much as crack your face around me again, I'm gonna bust it wide open."

At this moment, as I was reluctantly feeling that it was imperative for me to intervene, a group of merchant-men and my men came on deck, chatting together good-naturedly. The tension was broken, and I, for one, was mighty glad.

The ship's officers, generally, were very good and very friendly. They had been hand-picked by Captain Olafson, whereas he had no chance at choosing his crew and, for the most part, he had to take anyone who would sign. The first officer was a Swede and, oddly, an extremely lazy one. He was constantly fretting over his crew, but he never quite got around to doing anything about it, and I doubt that he dared to try. We assigned him to one of the bridge guns and he was much interested in that for about two days. Then the newness wore off and he never went near it again.

The second mate was a very good ship's officer. It was his first trip on the *Scotty* and he did an excellent job. He was a Texan, had been a cowhand once in his life, but had taken to sea fairly early. Later on, when we were in the lifeboat, he handled the boat crew extremely well, keeping down hysteria and immediately posting a guard over the provisions and water and arranging the men as comfortably as possible in the boat while we conducted a thorough search for survivors.

The third mate had been torpedoed a short while before and he was now making his first trip as ship's officer. He was a cheery, wisecracking fellow, and he seemed to be very well satisfied with life in spite of his experiences and the fact that he had all his teeth pulled while ashore and then got his sailing orders before he could get his plates. He gloated over this misfortune with considerable satisfaction, pointing out that it was impossible to eat the chow anyway, and in his condition he was not tempted to try. The third mate gumming his gruel at chow provided our chief topic for amusing conversation, and the subject was given a variety of treatment that would have outdone a radio comedian.

The junior third officer was an old German, about fifty-five, unmarried, and with no known relatives. About the best that can be said for him is that he stood a bridge watch. He meant no harm, and I believe he was a capable sailor, but he stubbornly refused to obey orders.

It was then the responsibility of the commander of the Armed Guard unit to enforce orders concerning darkened ship. The smallest light can endanger a ship, the lives aboard her, the cargo, and, in fact, a whole convoy. There is no help for it, the ship absolutely must be kept dark. I explained the situation to the junior third officer among others but he was not much impressed.

About midnight one night I noticed a flashlight moving along deck. I yelled, but the light merely kept on moving aft. I called to my watch on the after gun, and told him to "get that guy!" So, when the junior third mate reached the gun platform and started to climb up to the gun deck, the Navy man on watch just accidentally dropped a two-by-four on his head.

When I got back to the after gun deck he was out cold. I poured a bucket of water on him. The mate came to at once and he immediately demanded that the Navy man be thrown in the brig.

I took him up to the captain and reported the incident. Captain Olafson and his mates told the junior third to shut up and consider himself lucky. After all, the orders were to shoot anyone showing lights at night. I was a little sorry that the two-by-four treatment had to be given, but it did stop the showing of lights on that ship. I regret to say that we never saw the junior third mate again. He stayed away from us.

Most friendly of all were the engine-room officers. They had a genuine interest in the guns, and at least two of them were a little familiar with modern naval ordnance. Those officers were a great help to us.

One of the members of the ship's crew was a husky young fellow who had just been made a bosun. He was much impressed with his position, and he was a hard worker and did an efficient job with the crew, even though his manner constantly irritated the men. The bosun elected himself to responsibility for keeping the ship dark below, and every night this brought on a fight with one of the crew members who particularly detested him. The crew man would douse his lights just short of two-by-four treatment, and, while I first considered the possibility that we might have to toss him in the brig, I was always able to get him to turn out his lights a moment before the bosun was ready to punch him into insensibility.

Later we fished our light-burner out of the water, pulled him into our lifeboat, and I gave him first-aid attention and tried in every way possible to make him comfortable. He reciprocated this treatment by reporting, upon his return to the United States, that I had been the first one of the entire ship to get into the lifeboat. I am still looking for that guy and if I ever find him floating in the ocean I'll be tempted to push him back and look for a bigger one.

But our best friend on the *Scotty* was a big, ebony-skinned colored boy, whom we called Deacon and who worked in the steward's department. He was especially proud of "his boys" in the Navy gun crew, and he did everything he could to make their meals interesting and appetizing. Deacon could sing, and after his working hours he would make immediately for the Navy quarters to talk to the men off duty and to sing for them. I never had an opportunity to hear Deacon's songs, but, from the reports, he ought to have a good job in one of the Harlem spots when this war is over, and I expect nothing would delight him more. He is a real shipmate. He kept the men cheered during those first worrisome days when they were getting acquainted with the sea and their stomachs, and when the torpedoes got us and we took to the lifeboats it was Deacon, among all of us, who was able to think of jokes to get the men laughing. I saw him later in New York and he invited me to drop into one of the water-front bars with him and have a drink. I have never drunk with a better man.

The attitude of the members of the merchant crew constantly improved as we got to know them better. I think we might have become very good friends with all of them, as has happened on other ships, if the Nazis had not interrupted our little cruise—but I have been getting ahead of our story. . . .

14

By the end of our third day out we had a well-organized and effectively integrated crew, each man familiar with his gun and his duties. The merchant sailors who had volunteered for service on the guns were displaying genuine enthusiasm for the work, and, once the men had gone through gun drills together, a spirit of harmony prevailed. Our schedule of activity had been set up on a basis to keep the men busy and well exercised. When you consider that part of them are up on watch each night, the day's work was always rather heavy, but it was labor that needed to be done, and it was vital from the standpoint of morale.

A typical day's schedule, not including watches and drills, would include the following activities: check grease stores, check guns, check powder magazines (powder must be kept at proper temperature at all times), clean quarters, bedding, and personal belongings, paint the three-inch and five-inch guns and turrets, clean and paint the 20-mm. tubs, stands and plates (such work would be eventually finished, of course), check springs on all 20-mm.'s; clean three-inch ejector pawl, and check elevation and depressing gear on five-inch gun. Not all these tasks were done every day, but there were enough of them, added to the regular schedule, to keep all hands busy.

Shortly after going aboard I had studied the ship and drawn up the battle bill. I made a chart for the men that would indicate exactly where each should be when Battle Stations sounded. On our second day out we staged a battle drill, while I timed the men with a stop watch. It was then we learned the true significance of all the hurry in the training school. On shipboard—as anywhere else, but on shipboard particularly—any split seconds lost getting the guns into action may prove fatal.

If a man is asleep in his bunk, when General Quarters sounds, he must get into enough clothes to give him protection from the weather, dive through the narrow steel hatchways, negotiate the steep and treacherous ladders and show at his station in a period of seconds. He does this while the ship is rolling and pitching, and frequently he must make the last yards to the gun over decks awash with heavy seas. Just getting to battle stations is a job that is always arduous and sometimes dangerous.

Battle Stations is always exciting, for the men never know whether or not it is the real thing. But sometimes it is funny too. I remember the story we heard about an Armed Guard officer—I think he would prefer to remain anonymous— who took great pride in his ability to reach his station ahead of the men.

This officer cruised a good many thousand miles and a good many more soul-bruising watches and never once did he sight a submarine. Then he was ordered back to the

ATLANTIC

United States, and he took passage on a merchant ship. When Battle Stations sounded he was in his shower. He was not an officer of the crew, but he responded immediately. He grabbed a towel and ran naked into the passageway and started up the ladder. Just then a five-inch gun went off overhead and knocked him down to the lower deck. He ran to the port ladder and tried it again and the same thing happened and he was bleeding and covered with bruises. Finally he reached the main deck and someone immediately shoved a bucket into his hand and ordered him to bring drinking water for the crew. He was so busy he did not get to see anything.

Finally the battle ended and our officer, a mass of bruises and in the worst condition of all on the ship, went below for his clothes. He got on deck again just as a patrol plane came along, circled the ship, and dropped a note congratulating the crew and giving them credit for a submarine. After that our officer drew shore duty and, so far as I have heard, he has never got near a ship or a submarine since.

The third day we had a boat and fire drill. The fire drill went most heavily for the men below decks, who were organized into squads to man the valves or to prepare to cut away the bulkheads. My own crew members had the duty of preparing to flood the magazines. When boat drill sounded the crew swung the lifeboats out and then stood in their boat stations as their names were called out. The point in all the drills was for each man to know his proper place

113

and to be there in a minimum of time and regardless of what might happen. The lifeboat drills ran off with special smoothness. We had good reason to be glad of that before many more days had passed.

Early in the morning of our fourth day out, as I remember, we had our first opportunity to test-fire the guns. We tried five rounds on the five-inch, one round of solid shot on the three-inch, then three rounds of fuzed on each: the five, the four, the three. We finished up with twenty rounds on the 20-mm.

Everything worked perfectly, and we were elated. The guns sighted properly, as well as we could judge, they fired without difficulty, and the crews timed them well. We felt that we were ready for anything the Nazi submarines could furnish.

At about 1500 in the afternoon, with the sea running heavily and most of the men sick, we heard reports off our port beam that sounded like gunfire. I went taut as a fiddlestring and swung my glasses into the direction of the sound, ready to order General Quarters if the slightest reason arose. For a moment I had a horrible feeling that I wouldn't be able to make myself heard, but this quickly changed to a fear that my voice would start shouting regardless of my will. I was trembling and soaked with sweat. Still, without knowing exactly how, I managed to do nothing, which was precisely the right thing in the circumstances.

Then the sound of explosions renewed, unmistakable now, and I summoned the signalman, who was keeping his eyes on the freighter off our port bow, which would be the first to receive any message from the apparent trouble area.

But we saw no signal. We learned later that one of our escorts thought it had flushed something. It crisscrossed an area of ocean with depth charges and those were the sounds we heard. Whether they got the submarine, or whether it actually was a submarine, we didn't learn. But we were keyed for battle then. We knew that at last we were in the real thing.

Perhaps the night that followed was no blacker than usual, but it seemed so to us. For almost two hours we were pelted by a fierce rainstorm and visibility was almost zero. I made a tour of the watches to make sure the men were as comfortable as possible under the existing conditions. It was not a pleasant night. The sea was breaking over the main deck with a steady, relentless fury that pounded your breath away whenever you were forced to take it full on, and the wind drove salt spray into your mouth and eyes and nose until you were choked and helpless. It was not a bad sea, actually, and yet it seemed to me that the whole ocean was turning over, and we with it. What impressed me most was the steady, determined viciousness of the waves. They rolled in, broke across our bow, whipped down the deck in a spread of lashing foam and then, finding such a blow inadequate, came back with renewed strength to pound against the boat deck, to hurl tons of water across the waist of the ship, and to lick hungrily at the gun platforms. This cycle endlessly repeated itself, calm, dispassionate, but vicious. I thought of Joe Louis pounding an adversary, not hating him, but coldly determined to bring him down, measuring his punches to do just that job, but no more. I had a feeling that the impersonal sea was out to get us, but that the conquest would give it no particular satisfaction. I developed a sudden fondness for the good old ore-stained *Scotty*. She was rolling about twenty degrees, and she was pitching mildly, but even I knew that she was taking it easily in her stride, and that she was ready for more. The *Scotty* was a good boat, and that night I felt the need of a good boat under legs that couldn't quite get the feel of the sea.

I was wondering what the men were thinking, there on watch, trying to peer through the driving rain, blindly alert for danger they couldn't actually see but were somehow supposed to sense before it might be too late. I knew the tenseness, the grueling strain that comes to the watch. I knew the feeling you have when your eyes seem to bulge from their sockets and your nerves play you tricks and your hands refuse to control the glasses and you stand there quivering and afraid something might happen and yet hoping it will and wondering why, in God's name, you ever decided to get stuck on a boat.

All such sensations seemed familiar to me, but I wondered if all of the men had the same fears that I had, or if, perhaps, there was something wrong with me and I was not really one of them. That desire for oneness is strong in a man at sea. There is a unity in a ship's company you know nowhere else. You share the same food, the same shelter, the same experiences, the same life on shipboard as nowhere else, but still you can never be certain that another man's reaction is the same as your own. It's something like hearing sounds. When a violin plays or a siren screeches, what you hear and I hear is the same waves beating against similar timpani, but whether we actually both hear the same thing is something neither of us will ever know. Our structural differences may variously affect our sense of tone and pitch, and certainly the experiences we have had will give us differing connotative values. But I think that men on shipboard, when there are few of them and the strain is great, must come as near to sharing an experience on an equal basis as is humanly possible. Anyhow, that night prowling aft, with the sea in my face and tearing my hands from the lines we had strung, I felt very close to those men aboard and I was swept with such an emotion of affection for them as would have seemed maudlin at any other time.

It was in such a mood, which paradoxically was somehow joined with a general exasperation against the sea and everything it stood for, that I arrived at the after gun and was unable to see the watch. My first feeling was that he had been swept overboard. I yelled, and my cry was torn from my teeth almost before I could utter it.

Directly beside me there was an answering voice, and a very mild one, compared with my own: "Yes, sir, Mr. Berry."

He was so close it made me jump. More buckets of rain swept past, leaving in their wake a kind of vacuum, and in it I distinguished the outlines of the member of my crew, almost touching me. Uncertain of the merits of his sou'-wester, he had wrapped himself in the tarpaulin of the gun so effectively as to camouflage him completely and to obstruct partly his vision. I was so angry about my recent fear for him that I wanted to kick him in the pants. Technically, he was still at his post, so I delivered a little lecture that I felt should impress him. I explained that it was my responsibility to see that he was properly and warmly clothed for his duties, and that after that it was his job to carry them out, unencumbered by any tarpaulins.

"Yes, sir, Mr. Berry," he replied. He shook himself out into the rain and added, "But, sir, if any submarines come out on a night like this I think they deserve to have a shot at us."

The next day my watch, for lack of the boot in the pants, had extra duty in the way of swabbing decks and opportunity to meditate upon the vital need of keeping a taut watch regardless of conditions. I think, however, he would have preferred the boot.

15

The following morning the sea was calm, offering to us the variety of a clear, sunlit day, fresh crisp salt air, and pretty little whitecaps that played harmlessly in the distance. You'd have thought the night before must have occurred on some other ocean. We got back to our position in the convoy and returned to our drills at the guns with a feeling that everything was over and that from there on in it would be a nice, pleasant cruise.

It was Sunday, and we were taking it easy, but late in the morning I was assailed with a sense of restlessness. As I paced the bridge I got to thinking about Sunday mornings at home, when, after a special breakfast of ham and eggs, Mother would scrub down my two brothers and me, and dispatch the whole family off to church. Church hadn't meant much to me then, save when Christmas was approaching, but now, as I was thinking about it, and the memories of the hymns came flooding back, I felt a great comfort from my vision of our three well-polished heads in the pew, the voice of the minister, and the stately, calming rhythm of the choir. Suddenly it occurred to me that the men might have the same hunger for the comfort and stimulation of religion.

I approached Captain Olafson. "Sir," I said, "I was thinking that perhaps the men would like a chapel service on deck. . . . It's Sunday. . . ."

He looked at me a little surprised, and then his eyes twinkled. "Go ahead, Mr. Berry," he replied. "I think I would like it myself."

I wasn't sure how the men would take it, and I had a feeling that some of the tougher mariners among the merchant sailors would make it bad for those who did want to join in, but the idea still seemed good, and I was determined to try it.

There was a bit of room along midships, among the planes and tanks, and I sent out word that church services would be held at eleven o'clock, making it plain that attendance was purely voluntary. Then I hunted up my Bible, and tried to get clear in my mind the words of some of the hymns, because I knew that if a service was to be held I was going to be it.

At precisely 1100, six members of my gun crew—those not on watch—came out on deck, and they were followed by perhaps a dozen of the merchant crew members. Most of the latter were a little unsure of themselves and could not quite decide whether to participate. But I felt a thrill at seeing them. It seemed that my hunch was good.

When we were ready to begin, the blue and white flag of the church was run up to the main truck. We all stood there a moment gulping. There is only one time when another flag flies above Old Glory on an American ship.

That is the time when the flag of the church is flown while services are in progress. I looked up at the captain, and he smiled at me.

As I faced the men it was the most uncomfortable moment I had ever experienced. Speechmaking used to be a part of my job, but a speech at that time seemed mighty pointless. Those men, just by coming on deck, merely by the look in their eyes when the flag of the church was hoisted, were worshiping their God so honestly and with such sincerity that words seemed almost a desecration. I saw Jordan, our Bible reader, standing there watching the scene with glistening eyes, and whatever I had intended to say was swept away in a flood of emotion.

Still, there I was, and a service of some kind was in order.

"Men," I began finally, "I guess we all feel the same about religion and God and our fellow men, whatever our faith may be. That feeling, probably, is a little stronger out here. Religion is something real and genuine, something to tie to. It works best when you need it most. I am not going to try to talk to you about God, or about religion, because every man here knows as much about it as any other, and as little.

"We're out here because we feel something must be done about building the kind of a world religion contemplates. Probably most of us don't read the Bible very often, except for Jordan here, but in it are the plans for the kind of a world we all want, the kind of a world we're fighting for.

"I don't think any of you want to hear me say that God is fighting on our side. But I think He is with us when we are doing what we think is right and when we are doing a good job of it. A lot of great men have written down what they think God feels about the world, and about us. Whether these men were inspired by God Himself I don't know, but what they wrote is most certainly Godlike inspiration and I believe that the experience of humanity proves it to be what God thinks, as nearly as it is possible for human mind to conceive it. I think you can't do better than to read from those words:

" 'The eyes of the Lord are in every place, beholding the evil and the good.' "

The chapter, started at random, was finished, and we all joined in a hymn. Many of the merchant sailors were singing with us and we looked upon one another in full friendliness. I think that any resentfulness the old hands might have felt against us newcomers was gone then.

16

The day had grown very warm and after chow I went to the flying bridge in my shorts to take a sun bath. I was lying there comfortably when a commotion was observed among some of the ships of the convoy, and soon we got the signal of a submarine attack.

We immediately leaped to battle stations and manned all guns. Most of the men, like me, were stripped to the waist, and they stood tense about their weapons, their sweat glistening on their backs, waiting for the order that would send them into action.

We scanned the sea and could see nothing. The destroyers were darting all about the convoy, dropping depth charges, and the cumbersome freighters cut zigzag paths through the green waters.

We stood at our stations for two hours, watching and waiting. All that we got out of it was a good case of sunburn. Then we had a late cold supper and called it a day.

After that we all had a chipper feeling that the subs couldn't be so tough after all. That was twice they had been prowling about, and nothing happened. None of us was frightened or the least bit nervous during our two-hour alert. Our only anxiety was to do the job right if we got a chance for a shot. I know I was still too ignorant to be scared, and yet it was a welcome feeling—to survive an alarm without a particular loss of energy or a squeamish stomach. That night I went below at eight o'clock and turned in. It was the last time I tried that. Now if such an attack should occur I would post a double watch all night, and be up all night myself, resting on a cot on the bridge if there was a chance to rest at all.

The next day the convoy broke up, a number of us proceeding directly southward, and the rest turning west. We knew by then that we were bound for the Persian Gulf and that we would round Africa during the course of our journey. We knew also that we were in a dangerous zone. We began to get submarine warnings almost continuously, and the men practically lived at the guns. When there was little opportunity to go below for chow, Deacon would come galloping up, bearing a big tray of food and steaming coffee. The weather was hot, but we always welcomed the coffee. Or perhaps it was simply that we welcomed Deacon. He seemed to be completely unworried about the undersea menace.

"You boys will get 'em," he kept repeating, his black face split wide by a gleaming grin. "They ain't got a chance with you boys on them guns. I wouldn't give nothing for no submarine's chance. No sir."

Deacon's enormous faith in the crew and the guns inspired the men if they needed inspiration. His food and black coffee contented their stomachs. They badgered him unmercifully with their jokes, but he only grinned fondly at them and agreed with everything that was said. It was only when a man got a little homesick, or fed up with his job, that Deacon grew indignant.

"What's the matter with you?" he would demand. "Ain't you sailing around on one of the best ships in this ocean? Nothin' happened to you yet, has there? You got no call to be worryin'. The good Lord ain't goin' to let nothin' happen to us. You git a little food in yoah stomach, 'thass all th' matter with you."

And Deacon would force-feed them, if necessary, like a flock of Strasbourg geese.

At about 2200 that June night, we saw flares being shot into the air about two points off the starboard bow and a little later we saw a light blinking signals. This was a clear violation of the orders of the convoy commodore, and we didn't answer for fear it was a submarine and they would open fire on us.

We had a double watch that night, and it was an uncomfortable night. Whatever the signals might mean, a submarine was certain to be involved. If there was a sinking there was not a thing we could do about it. We could not stop to investigate. Our orders were to keep going.

By that time we had received sufficient warnings and hints of action to impress everybody aboard thoroughly. We were in the war zone, definitely, and at any minute we might be next. We felt that we were ready for them, and I don't think that any of us were frightened in the sense that we would have turned away from the danger if we could, but we certainly were not comfortable.

The men kept things going below decks with harmonica music and conversation as lively as they could make it. But a pall hung over us. A man would start a sentence and it would trail off into nothingness, as if something more important had come into his mind and what he had intended to say didn't matter anyway.

All of the men grew immensely considerate of one another. The extreme politeness and unselfishness might have seemed a little funny at any other time. We couldn't get rid of the feeling that the zero hour had struck and that something else might be striking very soon, only we didn't know when or where.

By morning the strain had started to tell on us. We wanted something to happen, anything. We felt it would be much better to be shot at, even to be hit, than to move along into unseen danger without being able to fight back. I suppose that the wear and tear on us is as nothing compared with what the men in subs must feel. Still, they are on the prowl. They are out looking for game. They can feel the exhilaration of sending the shot home. They are the hunters and they know they are pretty likely to get in the first blow. Looking for something to shoot at and then taking your chances in a fight seem to me to be one thing, while waiting to be shot at with no chance to take the offensive yourself is another. However, that is merely the point of view of one who rides above the waves. I would have no liking for the interior of a sub when depth charges are dropping close. I salute the men who do that hunting job which must be done, wherever they fight and under whatever flag.

The men in the engine rooms and the members of the black gang in our naval vessels and merchant ships also hold my complete admiration. The idea of being below decks when a torpedo strikes home and sets off a cargo of oil or TNT does not appeal to me. I prefer to take my chances on a clear jump from topside. But I have heard a good many engineers argue, quite vehemently, that the engine rooms are the safest part of a ship. How often, they demand, do you get a torpedo, one that smashes the bulkheads, before you have a chance to get clear? On the other hand, think of the chances you take topside with machine-gun bullets and antipersonnel bombs, and correctly fuzed shells. Only a man who is utterly foolhardy would prefer a station above decks if he had his choice, say the engineers.

That is one of the nice things about the Navy. Every man is wholly satisfied with his station, as compared to that of his fellows. You couldn't get him to exchange. He feels the profoundest pity for his mates and he is quite convinced that, whatever may happen to his ship, somehow he is going to squirm clear. I don't think that many men on our ships actually get scared, as we commonly think of it. They're too much fatalists for that. But they do get very uncomfortable and very cautious and if there is any choice they prefer to be as far away from danger as possible.

We had a feeling that our turn was coming, and soon. But the men went calmly about their duties. We really felt that we were ready for anything, and that all that was necessary was to keep cool. John Scott Clancy, another of our signalmen, summed up the situation. Clancy was on the bridge with me and we were discussing the proper conduct should a submarine suddenly poke its prow in our direction.

"I don't think I could possibly get excited any more," Clancy said. "These drills and this Navy routine have finally got me. I think that I can live the rest of my life strictly according to Navy Regulations. You know, if a submarine should surface right beside us and Hitler should stick his head out of the tower and say, 'Hello, Clancy,' my job is to go over to the speaking tube and calmly report: 'Object surfaced just broad on the starboard beam, sir.' That's all there would be to it."

I have a feeling that Clancy would forget Navy Regs just once and lean over and land a haymaker where it would do Hitler and everyone else the most good. He is a red-faced Irishman with blue eyes and sandy hair and a skin that blisters and peels constantly. He is the kind of fellow you like to have around when a fight is brewing. Clancy and I have sailed together since and I always like to lure him into talk, for he is one of the best conversationalists I have ever met. Before the war, Clancy worked as advertising manager for a public utility company in upper New York state. His publicity talents, plus his natural Irish blarney and his flair for showmanship make him a delight to hear. He is a fine man to listen to on a dead watch and he is an excellent signalman.

The day was very calm and we ran through our gun drills and fire drill. There was the usual inspection of decks, boats, guns, quarters and bilge. Everything appeared to be in order, and, as the day waned, I went about my regular business of inspecting the watches and making sure the ship was properly darkened. The watches now were of two hours' duration, each man to be relieved at five minutes before the hour. At night, however, the relief had to come up at least ten minutes before his duty began, to accustom his eyes to the darkness. Our watches were stationed in the forward gun emplacement, the No. 2 and No. 3 gun emplacements, and the after gun emplacement, in addition to the watch maintained by the ship's officers from the bridge.

The haze over the sea deepened. The sun, blood red in the west, finally dropped away completely and darkness came suddenly. The ship was heavy with shadows and the men, under their dull helmets, could be seen only with difficulty when they were but a few yards distant. The planes and tanks in their shrouds were mere huddled blobs of darkness, and finally they, too, seemed to disappear.

It was about 1900—seven o'clock—when I left Captain Olafson topside and went below to check on the blackout lights. I was going along a companionway two decks below the bridge when I felt a jolt that shook the whole ship. I was pitched sideways against a bulkhead. I knew immediately what had happened—you always know. I recovered, and felt that the ship had lurched in a direction away from the hit. I turned quickly to start for the hatchway when the second torpedo hit us. This time I was thrown forward on my face, the breath knocked out of me. I was stunned for a second, but then I got my wind back and I went for the door.

I seized the metal latch, but the door wouldn't budge. It had been jammed by the explosions. I had a very sick feeling, and in a split second saw in my mind's eye everything that had happened—the wake, cutting suddenly across the water out of nowhere, the cry of the watch, General Quarters sounding, the frantic work of the wheelman seeking to come about to avoid the blow, the men scrambling to their guns, the second crash and the dull explosion within the hull, the rush of water and the burst of flame. . . . Then I blanked out for a moment. I don't know whether I opened that door or knocked it out or went right through it. That I'll never be able to remember. But suddenly I was on the other side. There was what seemed to be a wall of water coming at me. The force of the explosions had driven the water up over the skin of the ship and down below the decks where it was rushing through the passageway. I threw out my hand blindly and my arm wrapped around

A NEW GUN AND PLATFORM

Gun platform and gun hoisted for installation on a merchant ship.

FINAL MECHANICAL TESTS TO GUN

a stanchion. I held on, blinded and suffocated, until my head cleared. Then I got my feet onto the ladder and climbed topside. It was not until then that I realized the ship was sinking fast.

On deck the action was almost indescribable, yet, as I have thought of it since, things were very orderly, everything considered. Men were at the guns, or rushing to them. The merchant officers were bawling orders to their crew, and the merchant crew members not scheduled for the guns were hurrying to their lifeboat stations. The ship was listing badly and men scrambling wildly across the deck would halt to secure their yellow life jackets, and then scurry on as madly as before, seeking their stations.

My station, like that of my crew, was with the ship. It was our job to get a shot at the submarine, and we knew that the Armed Guard usually gets its shot when the torpedoes are home and the waves are washing the decks. When the sub comes up for the finishing shots with her deck guns—then it's our turn.

I ran to the bridge and a man there was leaping up and down and yelling: "What'll I do? What'll I do?"

I still had the feeling that I was in the midst of a bad dream—that this couldn't happen to us. I didn't really think we were going to sink. But the sailor, with his yelling, brought me to reality.

"Get into your life jacket," I told him, while I raised my glasses and tried to sight the sub.

"What'll I do?" he yelled again.

I told him to take his glasses and look for the sub. I hadn't been able to see it, but I wanted to double-check.

The ship was sinking steadily, and I called to Captain Olafson, who was on the bridge below, and asked him if he was going to abandon ship. He answered that he was.

My crew was at battle stations. The after gun had been torn from its base and was swinging wildly. The men, mere pygmies beside that weight of lunging metal, were dodging on the platform, helplessly trying to do something with the gun. They were in immediate danger of being crushed. The machine-gunners were in position, hanging fast to their guns and gear in spite of the fact that on the port side they were knee deep in water. A tank pulled loose from its blocks and cables and went plunging across the deck.

I could see that if the men were able to get the after gun under control to the point of firing the piece, the recoil would probably drive the whole gun through the bridge.

I grabbed for the phone to tell the men to abandon ship. But the phones were gone. I yelled at the men to get to the lifeboats. They obeyed the order, but took their time. I had a thrill of pride in them. Our main gun gone, the decks awash, our deck cargo plunging at them, the ship threatening to blow up at any moment—still those men were ready to fight a submarine with their machine guns.

I watched them head for the boats. I didn't have any idea

where the merchant crew was by then, and at the moment I wasn't thinking about them. I heard a hiss of steam and a new thud of explosion below the decks and I was anxious for everyone to get clear.

One of the members of my crew started up the ladder toward me—Gallegos I think it was. I told him to get the hell out of there. He said that his lifeboat was smashed. I yelled at him to quit bothering me and to go to the first station he could find and get in.

Then I went below into the wheelhouse in search of Captain Olafson. He was struggling with his confidential papers scattered about him, attempting to cram them into a metal box so that they could be thrown into the sea. I knew well enough, of course, that it is necessary to dispose of recognition codes, cargo lists and similar confidential material, but by that time the decks were completely awash and I was furious that he should be wasting time trying to throw overboard something that was going to sink anyhow. I knew that a submarine crew will board an abandoned ship in search of just such papers and I knew they had to be destroyed, but, for the moment, the whole proceeding was exasperating.

I helped Captain Olafson stow the last of his papers. That done, he straightened up and looked at me in a bewildered fashion. He indicated with his arm that I was to clear out. It was obvious that he intended to remain with the ship. I felt that, temporarily, he didn't really know what he was doing. The engines were stopped, and save for the crackling of flames it was now very quiet. The *Scotty* righted herself and began to settle evenly in the water. It was time we were getting out.

I forced the captain into a life jacket, and then made a dash for my cabin, got my own jacket, sun helmet, flashlight and knife, and a handful of cigars.

Then I caught up with Captain Olafson, who was going down the ladder to the main deck. We waded through water up to our thighs to get to the boat deck. I went with the captain to his boat station and left him there. Then I made a hurried check around the boat deck and found one of my men—I don't remember now who it was. He was wandering about dazedly. I grabbed him and went to the port side with the intention of getting us both on a raft. The raft already had seven men aboard and it looked rather crowded, and the Navy man with me roused himself and held back. I had to push him into the raft and he was pulled aboard just as it swung clear of the ship.

Captain Olafson was still standing where I had left him. The boat at his station had already been lowered and the men had just cleared the falls. They threw us the lines that hung from the davits so that we could swing down into the boat. I grabbed one line, swung clear, and then noticed that Captain Olafson missed his. I think he missed it deliberately, believing that they would not be able to get both of us into the boat.

I still had a good grip on my rope, so I swung back, trying to grab the captain's life belt in order to pull him overboard into the boat. He pushed my hands away and before I could make another grab the ship heeled over and a boom cracked against my head. I went down into the sea. The cold salt water brought me to in a hurry. I came up into a pool of thick tar and foul-tasting fuel oil. Through my mind flashed a quick prayer, thanking God the stuff wasn't aflame.

I swam what seemed an interminable distance and then someone pulled me into the boat and dumped me on the bottom. I learned later that it was DuQuoin, our assistant engineer.

There was considerable confusion in the boat. It was very dark, and the ship in sinking had made up a heavy sea immediately about us. I had always heard about the suction, and why I wasn't pulled down I'll never know. Probably it was because the *Scotty* went under with such comparative gentleness.

The lifeboat was bobbing up and down like a cork. The planes that had been part of the deck cargo broke loose under the water and they kept popping up to the surface. One of them popped right beside us and we were scared stiff for a moment, until we knew what it was. The fuselage rose clear of the water, until the nearest wing was above our boat. Then it began to tip. We were afraid that it was going to sink us, but the men got the oars out and managed to push it away. Just then another lifeboat came up and rammed us a good hefty belt amidships. We lurched to starboard, and took water, until there were about five or six inches in the bottom of the boat. That didn't seem to bother anyone just then.

Suddenly it was very quiet on the ocean. No noise—save for the sounds of the men—not a ripple of water. It was actually calm and peaceful and the darkness lay over us like a blanket of black velvet.

For that brief moment it seemed that nothing really had happened. There was a second when even the voices of the men were stilled. I was unable to think for that instant, and had the sensation that I was just waking from a nightmare.

Then nervous reaction set in and all of us except Tex, the second mate, and me, became extremely nauseated. The men were sick all over the boat. I began to get scared. I shook so hard I couldn't hang to an oar. I remember that my stomach was drawn up into such a tight knot I couldn't have vomited if I'd had to.

After a few minutes of this Tex got his bearings first and said: "All right, dammit, there's work to do. Let's get the oars out and row around and see if there's anybody floating in the water."

That snapped the men out of it. They were glad to have something to lend a hand to. We put the oars into the locks, fashioned a couple of grommets with bits of rope, and the men started rowing feverishly. We rowed around for about an hour and a half, and picked up three men—no mean achievement in the darkness. Fortunately for us the sea was calm. Then we saw the other lifeboat and the life raft. We tied all three together, and then rested our oars for the night.

17

All of the men wanted to smoke, but we were afraid to permit it because the submarine might surface and machine-gun the boats. The men grumbled a little about this, but we were all equally aware of our danger and no one attempted to light a match.

There was very little talking, just a bit of wondering who was there, who wasn't, and how long we would be out. We didn't know where we were, of course.

Some of the men were hurt, but there were no complaints. Occasionally there would be a stifled groan as someone shifted his weight, or one of his mates leaned against him. But to every question I put there was the same answer: "I'm okay, sir."

We lay there in silence for a time, each thinking our own thoughts. I was wondering about Anne, and what she would think when the news came through. I hoped that we would make it all right and that I would be with her when the baby came. I was certain we would be found and my greatest concern at the moment was that she might worry needlessly.

Then someone would raise his voice against the silence: "I wonder if Peterson made it."

There would be a long silence as we reconstructed in our

minds those exciting last moments of the *Scotty,* and a voice would say: "I saw Peterson at his station. I guess he made it."

Some one asked: "Did the captain make it?"

I said: "No."

Someone said: "I was on the boat deck . . ." Then he stopped abruptly. Perhaps a few seconds later he would continue: "I was on the boat deck when she hit." He would stop again and everyone would be too weary and too preoccupied with his own thoughts to urge the speaker on.

After a while we felt better, and each man began recounting what he had done.

One had been knocked from his bunk. He grabbed for his pants, missed them, and showed up at his gun wearing only a pair of shorts. I thought about the sun that would hit us tomorrow.

"Hell," said another man. "I didn't even have shorts on. Goddammit, I'm naked!"

There were a few chuckles at that.

"I was below in the engine room," said one of the merchant sailors. "When she hit I was thrown to the deck. I knew right away what was happening. . . . I got up. I could sort of see the bulkheads opening, in my mind's eye. I remembered the escape ladder in the big ventilator. . . . Good thing I remembered that. I climbed up. Some bastard had left the screening on the ventilator. I kicked it out. . . . I wonder how th' hell I managed to kick it out? I guess I

must of cut this leg then. . . . Then I got over to the lifeboat."

The men agreed that the lifeboats had been lowered in
orderly fashion. At least one boat had been smashed by the
torpedoes.

The men began to compare notes on how frightened they
were. There was no pretending. Any man in that boat who
denied feeling fear would have been recognized at once as
an idiot or a liar. "Only me and my laundryman will know
how scared I was," one man said.

Over in the other boat I heard Deacon talking. His was
the only voice I could hear at the distance.

"If they'd of showed up you boys would a shot 'em," he
was saying. "You'd of fixed 'em," he added with confidence.
"You most certainly would have fixed 'em."

That made me wonder about the submarine. No one
had seen her surface. We were all certain she had not surfaced, and there had been no sign of her since the two torpedoes. She must have sighted us at a tremendous range.
The skipper of that sub wasn't taking any chances. He just
got out his plotting board and figured out where we were
and where he was and then he had the gyroscopes set and
the torpedoes went out on a collision course from perhaps
two miles away. That would be some shooting and I could
have genuinely admired it if only we had got a chance to
shoot back.

I began to wonder what kind of a report I would have to

turn in. I could see it: "From: Lt. (j.g.) Robert B. Berry. To: The Commandant. Subject: *Scotty,* sinking of."

I thought I would obtain the services of a competent yeoman when I made out that report. I would have liked very much not to make out any report at all.

Someone in one of the boats started singing softly: "Blest be the tie that binds." He repeated the line and then gave up abruptly.

Toward morning it grew cold, or so it seemed. I suppose it was a combination of sea water and fatigue. I began to be worried. If any of the men were badly hurt, the long night would do them no good. But no one admitted to injuries. Sometimes I thought I heard a sharp sigh, or a sob.

It was impossible to move about in the boat. I knew that we had emergency rations and a first-aid kit and gear for the management of the boat, and casks of water, for we made regular inspections. But there was no way to examine the men to discover if anyone needed help, nor give him assistance if he did.

18

When morning came we were a sorry-looking spectacle. Men were there with no clothing, in shorts, in pants and no shirts, and shirts but no pants. I was completely covered with a thick gummy coating of oil combined with salt. It seemed to eat into my sunburned skin. It was weeks before I got it all off.

One of the men had got oil in his eyes. The pain must have been bad during the night. His eyes were swollen and rheumy. I broke out the first-aid kit and swabbed his eyes with boric acid, and he said they were all right, although he could scarcely see. Two or three other men had cuts and scratches but there did not seem to be any serious injuries among us. So, after the application of first aid, we dealt out a drink of water and a piece of chocolate to each man, passed around some cigarettes that had escaped wetting, and everyone had a good smoke. The cigars I so thoughtfully brought I had tossed away during the night when the mixture of decomposed tobacco, salt water and fuel oil in my pocket attracted my attention.

While we smoked there was a slight commotion in the second lifeboat as Rollins, one of the merchant sailors, reached beneath a thwart and produced his cat. Rollins calmly ignored the stares of his mates while he attempted to share his piece of chocolate with the puss, and when she, after a couple of exploratory licks, disdained the delicacy, Rollins ate it himself. It was not, however, until he offered the cat a drink from the common cup that there was any protest.

"My God," yelped one of the engineers, "ain't we got troubles enough without sharing our water with a damn cat?"

Rollins looked up defiantly. "That's my water she's drinkin'," he said quietly. "She's cleaner than you are."

"We had to hold up the damn boat so he could go back an' git her," the engineer called to us.

Then everyone sat quiet, contemplating Rollins and the cat. None of us was hungry, nor did we expect to be, but I think the same idea struck all of us at once.

"You will like hell!" said Rollins. He chucked the cat back under the thwart. Then he grinned and everyone began chuckling. I learned later that he actually had risked his life to save the cat when Abandon Ship sounded.

We were not in bad condition. Our lifeboat was one of the large, whaleboat types, with air tanks for stability and sufficient freeboard to keep us from being wet by the sea. It had been well provisioned, and had a fair amount of gear aboard, including a sail and compass. We set a course of about 210 degrees True, judging the nearest land to be in such direction, although we did not really know where we were, and there was no sun-shooting equipment aboard. We hoisted our sail and arranged a schedule at the oars, but we took it easy on the rowing, for we felt it would be better to conserve our strength than to attempt to reach land in a hurry. We knew that we were not far off the patrolled routes, and that sooner or later a plane should find us.

When the sun began to appear we were heartened, for we felt certain we were proceeding in the right direction. As the sun rose higher, however, a new worry developed. At least half the men were unclothed above the waist and bare skin could not stand those searing rays for long.

Still, most of us had not been much harmed by our experience when Tex, who was acting as lookout at the time, yelled that he saw a plane to the southwest. There was a loud demand for proof from both boats and the raft. Look as we would, not a man of us was able to discern the speck in the sky that Tex had seen.

After that first disappointment our spirits hit bottom. We bent to the oars in silence for a moment. Then someone started to sing:

> "She'll be comin' round the mountain when she comes!"

In the middle of the song, Tex signaled for silence. "Listen, goddammit!" he demanded. "There is a plane!"

The singing stopped at once, and every eye strained across the coppery expanse of sea and sky in the direction Tex was sighting. I thought I could hear the sound of motors. The men began talking again, hopefully now, and I called for silence. Then we all heard it. The faint but unmistakable drone of a plane.

Everyone cheered and a couple of men in their excitement tried to stand up in the raft. It threatened to capsize, and they were yanked down. By that time the patrol plane was clearly in view. She circled us a couple of times, and dipped her wings to indicate she had seen us. Then she started off in the direction we were moving, wagging her wings in sign that we were on the right course, and in a moment she had disappeared to the westward.

Our lifeboat voyage was a picnic after that. We rowed to keep busy, but the sea was calm and we were in no greater danger than most Sunday visitors at Coney Island, who always succeed so beautifully in collecting a nice, first-degree sunburn.

At about eleven o'clock we saw a smudge on the horizon and we knew that the plane had given our bearing to a ship. At about 12:30 we could see it. We put in a frenzied half hour of rowing, but neither the ship nor our little convoy appeared to make any progress. But by 1400 (two o'clock) our rescuer was alongside, and we were taken aboard.

She was a merchantman, slightly smaller than the *Scotty.* I immediately reported to the captain, and told him that there were other lifeboats in the vicinity. This information he had already received from the plane, and he did not seem pleased to have me reiterate it. He made it plain that he desired to get out of that vicinity as rapidly as possible. His manner seemed to indicate that it was doubtless our own fault we had been torpedoed and the least we might have done was to row ashore without endangering another vessel by permitting ourselves to be found.

There was considerable confusion aboard, with everyone obviously experiencing a bad case of jitters. The Navy gun crew on our rescue ship was occupied at its tasks, and the merchant sailors were either too busy running about, or too worried, to pay much attention to us. Some of the men from the *Scotty* began to show signs of fatigue and shock, so I herded them below, made them strip, and started an examination for serious bruises and possible internal injuries.

19

I called roll as the men went off to find bunks, or a shaded spot on the deck where they could rest, and discovered that we had lost four men besides the captain—all of them members of the merchant crew.

As soon as the men had been cared for, Lieutenant (j.g.) Kammerer, commander of the gun crew aboard our rescue ship, and I began to check the life-saving facilities. Our radio was working and was constantly receiving warnings of submarine activity in the vicinity. We now had 181 men crowded aboard and I had reason to know what might happen should there be a rush of too many men to too few lifeboats if the U-boats struck again. We found that there were two lifeboats and four rafts, each with a capacity of eighteen men, in addition to one boat and a raft from the *Scotty*. The two other boats we had brought over had been secured to the ship by breast lines and sea painters, but the job was ineptly done and they had broken loose and drifted away.

At 1600 (four o'clock), Lieutenant Kammerer and I called up the men from the rescued crews and stationed alert watches all over the ship. We worked out life stations for all the men aboard, and we ran through a hasty drill. By 1800 radio reports of submarine activity against a near-by convoy indicated that we were entering an area of special danger. All of us were too excited to eat.

At about 1930 the speed of our ship was suddenly reduced. I ran to the bridge and the captain informed me that navigation conditions and trouble with the engines forced the three-quarters speed. I was worried then, because it was obvious that by now we were in the region of greatest submarine activity, and, at a speed of only six knots, we would be easy game for any undersea craft that might come along.

We were well equipped with guns aboard, and would have a good chance of making a fight of it if attacked, but our speed was such that a submarine might score a hit at a great distance. I could vision the mooring-board problem that would be offered, and could see the little line that would be drafted, plotting a collision course for a torpedo and our ship. It would be like shooting clay pigeons in a goldfish bowl.

The feeling that we were trapped swept over all of us, including the captain. We were running a zigzag course, but all of us believed that it was a mere matter of time until we would have to fight or be sunk. We were ready and willing to fight, but the prospects didn't seem too good that we would ever have a chance.

Shortly after 1930 Lieutenant Kammerer asked me to man the bridge telephones while he went aft to make an inspection of the guns and watches. The next half hour was one of the worst I have ever experienced. My body did not seem tired, but my eyes were ready to burst from their sockets and I was constantly starting with fear as I saw imaginary objects in the water. We had received more radio warnings and by that time I was convinced that we were sailing into a pack of subs. I was sure that one split second's failure to report an object might prove fatal. But the harder I tried to remain alert the tougher it got.

A little after 2000 (8:00 P.M.) I noticed a sliver of light shining a considerable distance astern of us and the shock of that had me wide awake. I called the captain's attention to it and while we were trying to decide what it was and its distance from us, the light suddenly grew brighter and then went out. A few moments later we heard the sound of an explosion in the distance and we assumed that another ship directly astern had been hit.

We immediately altered course, but did not change speed.

Now, at least, we were reasonably sure where the enemy was and that the attack would come soon. The ship was alerted and the men were ready at their guns. The moon, white and round above the water, was full upon us and we knew that we were a perfect target despite our darkened ship.

We moved along slowly for a terrible hour. There was no doubt that we would be next, but no one could guess for certain the direction from which the torpedo would come. If the submarine took it easy we could expect trouble on our port, but, our speed being what it was, the Nazi commander could maneuver for any position he chose, since his speed would be greater than ours.

At 2100 the moon slipped under heavy clouds. We sent up quick prayers of thanks. This at least would tend to make the battle more equal, although, in a way, the moon-light had provided us with some of the advantages it gave the sub. However, we were really not looking for the sub. We were trying to run away, at six knots an hour! We would be content not to see the sub at all, so long as it didn't see us. But if there was to be an exchange of looks, we wanted to have ours first. Considering that the sub probably was listening to us on his sound devices already, while we possessed none, our hope for a first look was rather futile.

When the moon disappeared I went far out on the bridge to gain every benefit for my eyes I could. I was perched there, glasses to my eyes, my nerves like pulled wires, my head throbbing with strain, when I heard the captain shout:

"Here she comes!"

Then it hit, on starboard midships.

My only thought was: "Goddam, now we've got to do it all over again!"

"Cast loose the life rafts," the captain yelled. He blew his whistle to abandon ship.

The water was still spraying down from the explosion. I felt no shock.

"Keep those life rafts!" I shouted.

I had a feeling that this time the submarine was going to

surface and that we were going to fight and I wanted at least one raft aboard to take the men away How the fight must end we all knew well enough. We were hit first.

I searched for a periscope to starboard and thought I saw something and called the elevation and bearing to the guns. I heard the numbers repeated. Then something happened, and I have never been able to learn what it was.

Probably it was the recoil of our five-inch gun. One of the Navy gunners in the turret above came hurtling down. His body caught me and we both went through the hatchway below. I was practically strangled by telephone wires and was cussing at the top of my voice and demanding to know what had happened. The gunner didn't bother to answer. He picked himself up, pulled some wires free, and dashed to the main deck intent on regaining his gun station.

I was too confused by the fall to make my fingers work nimbly and it was some time before I got the wires completely untangled. Then I started on a tour of the ship. We did not seem to be sinking and by that time I was too mad to think of being frightened or of the problem of abandoning ship. I was looking for gunners because I could see that the after gun was in good condition and I could also see the sub surfaced and cruising about the ship some five or six hundred yards away.

But orders had been given for all hands to abandon ship and they had been obeyed. There was the gun and there was a submarine and after our two experiences I knew there wasn't a man from the *Scotty* who wouldn't have risked a salt bath for just one good shot. But it was too late for such thoughts then.

By this time the submarine had opened fire on the ship with her deck gun. The first shot was high and went screaming over the mast. The second fell short, but the third plowed through the boat deck and I thought it was about time to get going. I ran to starboard and found only a dangling lifeboat that had been smashed by the explosion. I tried the port side and saw a boat just pulling away from the ship. I yelled and someone shouted: "This boat's full."

"To hell with that!" I answered. "I'm coming in."

The boat was overcrowded and several of the men were hurt. The mate in charge was third officer of the ship. He was doing his best, but the men were too closely packed and the injured were in the way and he could not get the oars into action.

We were between the submarine and the ship, and the ship was still under way, and the churning screw almost got the lifeboat. Then the sub opened fire with machine guns, and the tracer bullets screeched past us.

This started a panic in the lifeboat. The mate, who evidently knew little about boats, issued orders to his crew members and they told him to go to hell. The reason for their frenzy, I discovered later, was that they knew what cargo they were carrying, and the submarine's deck gun had started several fires.

Our danger was great. There were six members of my crew from the *Scotty* and they were ready to take orders and get out of there. I ordered them to move the injured clear so we could work. Then I crawled aft to where the mate was sitting, drew my gun, and threatened to shoot the first man who refused to obey orders.

The oars were broken out in a hurry and the boat began to move. Then we dug up more oars and I got on one of them with a merchant sailor, while the mate gave orders. Inexperienced or not, he knew more about a ship's boat than I did.

We quickly made headway and got out of the line of fire from the submarine, which poured between forty and fifty shells into our ship from her deck gun and then sent two more torpedoes home. I tried to learn whether we actually had got a shot at the sub from our after gun, but no one knew.

We rowed for almost three hours, until we were ready to drop with fatigue, circling the site of the sinking in search of other survivors. We took three more men aboard, making a total of forty-seven.

During this time a second submarine surfaced, about two miles away, and the Germans on the two U-boats talked to each other by blinker. Two of the men from our ship were still swimming and when they came close to the nearer sub an officer standing on the conning tower called to them in perfect English and told them that there was a life raft floating near by. Then he pointed out the raft with his search-light. A little later he approached the raft and told the men that there were several swimmers near by and he pointed them out with his light.

Then he called, "So long and good luck," and the subs departed.

20

During the time we cruised for survivors the ship was ablaze from several fires started by the shelling and from a big fire deep amidships that had been caused by the torpedoes. The sea about the ship was lurid with flame and bits of burning debris tossed off from time to time hurtled through the skies like skyrockets. We were perhaps two and a half miles away when she seemed to decompose before our eyes and a great red glare burst against the night. Then we heard a low, dull thud that seemed to keep vibrating in our ears long after we had felt the sound. The stern of the ship raised in the water and she rolled and slid under the water, with firebrands popping into the air until they were hid by clouds of steam that finally dissolved into the waves. It became very dark on the ocean.

After the ship had gone down we stopped rowing and floated around. The men who were hurt were having a bad time and we made them comfortable as best we could. The second sinking within twenty-four hours had a curious effect on my men and me. We were neither sick from shock nor afraid. We were just mad and disgusted. We spent the night moaning about the fact that we didn't have a chance for a fight. That the ship might well have exploded in fifteen minutes didn't alter the situation. We knew that she didn't go down for almost four hours and we could have pounded out a lot of shells in that time.

When daylight came we began rowing again, for we felt that we were near land and some of our men were in need of medical attention. The sun came out very hot, but we had not been caught without clothing this time, and most of us even had helmets.

The boat was terribly overcrowded. It was built for thirty-six men and we had forty-seven aboard. It was necessary for all hands who were able to take turns standing. As the sun got hotter and the men grew wearier there was a lot of grousing and grumbling and I knew that if help didn't come quickly we were in for a lot of trouble.

At about 1030 we came upon another lifeboat with a raft in tow and we secured our craft together. Neither the boat nor the raft had water aboard, so we shared our supplies. The merchant mate in charge of the boat told me this was the sixth time he had been torpedoed. We could not transfer any of our men to the other lifeboat, for it was almost as overcrowded as we were. We were very lucky that the sea was calm. We never could have survived a storm. As it was, men were passing out from the heat and it was almost impossible to clear enough space to help them.

We held a council of war across the boats and decided we could probably make the Venezuelan coast. We got out the charts in the lifeboats, decided what our position might be, did a little dead reckoning on the distance we might have

156

THE DAWN BRINGS A DULLER JOB

Cleaning the muzzle of a five-inch gun the day after a night of action is the necessary but not so glamorous duty of the seamen.

SHELLMAN, READY TO INSERT PROJECTILE

gained while circling through the night, and plotted a course that we hoped might take us shoreward. We dared not think of what would happen if our course was wrong. If anything started a panic on the raft or the boats it would be the end of us. I kept my gun on the transom between my legs.

At about noon we sighted smoke to the southwest.

"If that's a merchant ship I'm damned if I'm going to get aboard," one of the men said. "I'd ruther take my chances in a lifeboat. Even this 'un."

It was, however, a small Navy patrol craft, which came over quickly to pick us up.

It had no medical officer and I went below with the men to do what I could for them. Then I looked up the commander. That Navy crew was wonderful. They turned over their quarters and broke out food and clothes and made everyone feel immediately that, by heaven, the United States Navy takes care of its men. As for me, the skipper looked me over and said: "I suppose you want a bath and some clean clothes?" So he sent me to his cabin and had them get out a quart of medical-issue Scotch and said: "Help yourself." I took a drink, and undressed, and took a drink, and shaved, and took a drink, and took a shower, and took a drink, and put on a pair of shorts, and then I took a drink and remarked that this was a mighty nice ship. Finally I got dressed and called in the officers of the merchant ships that were aboard and gave them what was left, but there was no danger they might become intoxicated.

When I went topside they had sighted another raft. This one bore Gallegos and the crew of fifteen merchant sailors he had picked up during the night. I got a pair of glasses on them and saw it was Gallegos with his knife in his teeth.

I have never before had such a thrill of pride as I felt when he stepped aboard and saluted and I saluted him and shook his hand. I felt pride in the whole United States Navy but Gallegos was not much impressed.

"I'm tired, Mr. Berry," he said. "Can I go to sleep?"

21

We lost about sixty men in the second sinking, most of them from the merchant crews of two ships, several from the gun crew of the second ship, and one from my unit of the Armed Guard. We didn't speak of the losses, for it was possible that the men had been rescued, and if they were still floating out there somewhere on a raft or lifeboat, none of us wanted to think about it. Our own man, whom we knew best of course, was Brown, a lad from Tennessee. He was a quiet, likable chap who did his job and hoped to go back to railroading when the war ended. I have never learned what happened to him. As in the case of the first sinking, we again lost our captain. Neither he nor the first mate was ever found.

That night all of us who were able worked with the Navy crew. We were still in submarine territory and we had the survivors of three torpedoed ships aboard, which was far too many men. The skipper put on a double watch everywhere and we plowed through the night toward the nearest port, which was a good distance away. In the morning—it was Wednesday and I hadn't slept since Sunday morning—I went below to chow and sat at the table and went to sleep. That was at six o'clock, and I slept until noon while all the officers breakfasted around me and then returned to join me for lunch. Then I woke up and began eating without realizing until later I had lost six hours.

The trip to port was uneventful. I reported to the Port Director, got medical attention and barracks space for my crew, and went into the curious little town to get some clothes. The shirt, pants and shoes I had acquired through the good offices of Lieutenant Kammerer were already in bad condition.

The stores in town had nothing big enough to fit me and the merchants seemed to be in some doubt that I could pay for anything I might want anyway. I was never sure that I was seeing all their wares. Finally I met an officer who took me to the British supply base and I picked up some clothing at the British Vitteling store, an institution something like our Ship's Service stores. The officer in charge was very considerate, opening the store, which had been closed for the day, and persistently hunting through his stocks until he found something that would fit. Also he charged me the regular British navy prices for the supplies he could provide. I next went to the U.S. Army Engineers' supply store and obtained khaki shirts and pants. There the officer in charge told me to take what I needed and to forget about paying for it if I didn't have the money.

In town the news of the torpedoings had got about and I heard reports that the merchant sailors had refused to go back by ship and that they were demanding to return to the United States by plane. The seamen were royally received, and while we were in town the American civilian workers on the Navy base raised a purse of $2,000 for them, and the Red Cross provided them with food and clothing.

I had been in port but a few hours when I received orders to return to the United States by Navy transport plane. Riding out to report at the Naval Air Station I saw an officer who looked familiar. I looked again, and recognized him as Tommy Billion. Tommy had lived near me in Sioux Falls, and had been a classmate in medical school at the University of South Dakota. I hailed him and was able immediately to abandon the role of a lonely, shipwrecked sailor. Tommy took me to his room, lent me one of his suits, and hunted up his can of red paint.

"Come on," said Tommy, "you deserve to have a time. I've got liberty and an invitation. Come on, we're going down to a swimming party."

For a moment Tommy couldn't understand why I declined.

22

After reporting in at the Armed Guard Center in New York I was given leave and I hurried home to Anne. My cablegrams had told her there was nothing to worry about but I had not been too sure that all was well with her. When I saw Anne I knew, finally, just how scared I was when the *Scotty* went down.

["You should have seen him," Anne Berry said. "If I didn't love the guy I would have thrown him out. He was wearing a pair of wrinkled, too-small pants, a foul split-pea green shirt he'd picked up somewhere, and an English petty officer's cap two sizes too little. He had a laundry bag with his life belt strapped around it and an overnight kit with a broken strap. Such a woebegone sight I never expect to see again. Inside the bags he had the shirt and pants he wore when the *Scotty* went down. What with salt water, sand and oil they were so stiff you could stand them in the middle of the floor and climb them. He also had a coconut, an orange, some English shorts and the socks that go with them, the hunting knife he was wearing about his neck when they were hit, a few souvenir coins carefully wrapped in some dirty undershorts, two bottles of Scotch and a bottle of rum. But I was mighty glad to see him."]

We had five splendid days. Then Anne generously agreed

162

to give up half the leave to permit me to see my folks in South Dakota.

My trip across half the country made me anxious to get back to sea. Many of the people I met appeared neither to know nor to care that there had been a Pearl Harbor. The bitching I heard about coffee and gas rationing, the shortage of sugar and the mistakes of the government, the headlines I saw about strikes and the demands for "business as usual" left me a little sick. Men told me, with great authority, that reports of sinkings of merchant ships off our coasts were just a lot of propaganda. I hoped that Faustin Gallegos and his mates, and the thousands of others like them, would not meet such people.

I knew of course, that the little, noisy, cheap persons are not those who represent America. I saw that convincingly when I received my next assignment. I saw then that the grousers and complainers didn't count and the battle of production was being won by a nation that was wholly and completely in the war. And when you are sailing the seas, where the subs are waiting to pot you, it is good to know that.*

---

* On August 20, 1942, Lieutenant (j.g.) Robert B. Berry was commended by Secretary of the Navy Frank Knox "for skill and bravery shown by you as officer in charge of the gun crew during these encounters. . . ."

Part II

PACIFIC

1

WHEN I reported back at the Armed Guard
Center I was told to pick up a crew and proceed to another port where our ship was being
fitted.

My crew looked as if it had been selected by the League of
Nations. Charbula, Ashe, Murphy, Pezzulo, Amendolara,
Baujan, Marzinski, Mueller, Armstrong, Benoit. . . . I called
the roll and was thinking in the back of my mind, by
heaven, this is America! We had sixteen men and a petty
officer and we picked up two signalmen later. We represented everyone through our lines of progenitors—Allies,
Neutrals and Axis. But we represented only one main idea:
We wanted to kick hell out of the Japs and Germans and
there were some among us who had a special yen for boot-
ing the followers of Mussolini as well. Those Italian lads
among us, from Brooklyn every one of them, were strictly
out for fight and their notions never once changed during
the long months of our cruise. I could never quite determine
why it was that the Italians in Africa were always surrender-
ing while our lads, one generation removed from the soil of
Italy, were as good fighting men as I had ever seen. I think,
probably, that the ideas a man has in him determine what

he will do under fire. For a fighting, hard-working crew, you can give me Italian-Americans any time.

We had a good crew any way you looked at it. Four of the men previously had served at the guns, others had been to sea before, and two of them had been torpedoed. Since I had gained a little experience myself, I decided that we would be in good shape for anything the enemy could offer.

When we reached our port a fine surprise awaited us. We were to have a new Liberty ship, the *Roberts*,* just completed. We went down to the docks immediately to look her over. She was clean and big and particularly designed for the tasks ahead of her. We went aboard and I gloated over the smell of paint and tar that hung about her, recalling the less pleasant odors that first greeted me aboard the *Scotty*. There is nothing nicer than the smell of a new ship and her gear cooking in the sun. It's as wholesome as salt air itself. Sniffing a fine, redolent coil of new line will whip up your appetite better than will a pungent whiff of sizzling steak. And our first glimpse of the mess told us we could work on our appetites and really let them go. I was sorry that Goodwin was not with us.

Much to my joy, I discovered that the guns had not been mounted. I turned over to Gilbert, our coxun, the task of getting the men established in their quarters, while I camped on deck to make certain the guns were installed the way we

---

* The real name of the ship is not divulged for reasons of security.

wanted them. I didn't want any more ready boxes welded down portside-to.

It wasn't long before the ship fitters and gunsmiths swarmed on board and the big cranes walked over with our new shiny five-inch dangling. I talked to the foreman and he agreed that the way to put guns aboard was the way the gunners wanted them. I couldn't quite believe that things could go so beautifully, but after I watched for a while and saw that the labor crews went at the work like men who knew their business my worries ended and I went out to look over the ship.

The spotless cleanliness everywhere was delightful, and I could see, inexperienced though I was, that the men who built Liberty ships had thought the problem out. There were big holds and big hatches, designed for big cargoes and quick, inexpensive loading. There was plenty of room for guns and consideration had been given to the men's need of protection. In the wheelhouse, gleaming and efficient-looking as the cockpit of a bomber, I discovered that our new ship could regularly do ten knots, as compared with the eight knots of the *Scotty*.

The *Roberts,* in fact, was ideally built for everything but the comfort of the men. The merchant-crew quarters were nice and clean, and reasonably large, but they were all constructed around the stack and directly over the engines, which meant that in warm weather it was almost impossible to enter them at all. In my own cabin the deck was always so hot I couldn't step on it with bare feet. The quarters for the gun crew were on the stern, just over the steering engines, and they likewise were insufferable in hot weather. We spent much of our time in tropic ports, and entering quarters in those regions was like walking into an oven. However, both the men and I slept at the guns most of the time, so quarters were merely required for stowage purposes anyway.

The *Roberts* looked to be very seaworthy, and actually she was. All Liberty ships I have seen, however, tend to be top heavy, particularly when they are carrying deck cargo, as we did, and I have never rolled more in my life than on that trip across the South Pacific. On the first leg of our journey on the *Roberts* all of our dishes were broken and we ended up using condensed milk cans for utensils. It was not uncommon for a man to eat with an arm locked about a stanchion. But, roll though they do, those Liberty ships can go places.

We were fitted out very speedily and had no difficulty getting supplies. Something certainly had happened to the supply situation since I first went to sea a few weeks previously. By the amount of food coming aboard we knew we would be out for a long time, unless the submarines again cut us short. Actually, however, we ran low on food before our voyage ended and we spent the last few weeks eating salt pork and bread without butter.

The guns on the *Roberts* looked specially good. There

was a five-inch on the stern, a three-inch dual-purpose on the bow, and a number of new 20-mm.'s.

Our new guns were a bit more complicated than those we had previously, so we immediately began drilling to train the trunnion operator and the loader in their particular operations. The trunnion operator elevates and depresses the hoist upon which the gun is mounted, to maintain the line of parallax with the deck and to provide the gunners with greater clearance in manipulating the weapon. The loader removes empty magazines and replaces them with filled ones—at automatic fire a full magazine can be emptied in ten seconds, so no mistakes on the part of the loader can be tolerated. After a few drills we were able to have our new-type 20-mm.'s in action within forty-two seconds from the time an alarm sounded. There are some gunnery officers who claim to be able to do it in thirty seconds, but I doubt whether it can be done under conditions of surprise attack.

While we were taking on cargo I scoured the port for exactly the kind of accessories we would require at sea. We had no trouble at all getting what we needed—ejector pawls, replacement barrels, spring holders, sponges, cleaning rods, and all the other little incidentals a gunner likes to have about him. In addition we came back from our forays loaded with side arms, binoculars, spyglasses, gas masks, helmets, lanterns and flashlights, signal-light kits, asbestos gloves, and similar gear. I even managed to pick up an extra towing spar. The performance of those little sea pigs had impressed me so much on the previous trip I couldn't miss an opportunity to bring one aboard personally.

After we had fitted we journeyed up and down the coast picking up cargo. Those sorties demonstrated to us that we were really aboard a ship, and that, beyond all doubt, we had a captain. Captain Brown demanded that his command function shipshape and Bristol fashion. He had a crew that knew its business. These facts were a source of considerable comfort to us, for, by this time, we had guessed that we were in for a little business with the Japanese.

When the hatches were finally closed and the *Roberts* was far down in the water we thought that the time had arrived to shove off. Instead, however, we put into a port not far from the town where Anne was working and where we maintained our home.

We learned that we were to take PT boats aboard. The news created a lot of excitement on the *Roberts,* and in the port as well, for such craft had never been shipped out of an East-coast port before, nor had a merchantman loaded in that area for a trip into the Pacific. And our guesses about our destination had now become a conviction.

The day we anchored, carpenters came aboard to construct cradles for the PT boats and the following day the boats themselves arrived at the docks. My crew was delirious. We had heard all kinds of wild stories about rollercoaster rides in the PTs and about their fire power and their exploits in the Pacific and this was our first opportunity for a good look.

I was making an entirely informal inspection, admiring the intrepidity of the men who ventured to take such egg-shells into enemy gunfire, when I saw a naval officer approaching who seemed familiar to me. He was big and brown and hard and had on his face one of those cheerful grins that make you want to chuckle just seeing it. I was sure I had seen the fellow somewhere and I thought he looked exactly like Bob Montgomery of the movies.

He came over and introduced himself. "I'm Montgomery," he said. "Looks like they got 'em here all right."

"I'm Berry," I answered. "Looks like we're going some place."

Lieutenant Montgomery grinned. "You bet," he agreed. "We're going to have a helluva time putting these things aboard."

He was going to shepherd the squadron of PT boats across the Pacific and put them into action where they would do the most good. The news of his arrival, and the entirely correct scuttlebutt to the effect that he would be with us on the *Roberts,* completely eclipsed the excitement created by the arrival of the PT boats. . . .

[Here Anne Berry spoke up.]

"Bob, you've got to let me tell about Lieutenant Montgomery's visit. When he arrived the news got around in a hurry and every woman in town was agog. They kept seeing Robert Montgomery on every corner, and I'll admit that I was anxious for a glimpse of him myself.

"But did Bob Berry tell me that Lieutenant Montgomery was aboard with him? He did not. He talked about '*the* Lieutenant,' but I never guessed who was meant. All I heard about was the trouble everyone was having stowing some boats. One night Bob brought Captain Brown out for a drink, and then the two of them sat there all evening and discussed one thing—stowing boats. I remember that they had some idea of loosening the lines so that the boats could be put off to go chasing after submarines on the high seas. It scared me just to hear them talk about it.

"Then, the next night, Bob had the mate out to dinner, and he and the mate sat all evening discussing the stowing of boats. It seemed the problem was really unstowing them. The mate said that he was going to cut the stays with a hack saw so they could be broken out in a hurry when you ran into trouble.

"Then the next night someone else came along and there was a discussion about a scheme to arrange the boats so they would discharge torpedoes, and it was that night I think, that Bob came out with his plan, which combined the worst features of all of them. Anyhow, the general idea was that once you got to sea you were not going to wait for submarines to attack, but you were going out to get them with

174

the boats you were carrying. It all sounded very wonderful and a little bit insane.

"All that time, Bob Berry, you didn't say a word about Lieutenant Montgomery, but just kept referring to him as *'the* Lieutenant' and saying what a swell person he was and that he was mixed up in this madness about boats that would chase submarines.

"All that time I didn't guess, of course, that Bob was working right beside Lieutenant Montgomery every day. Downtown everyone was still talking about him, and the girls were wondering if it would be possible to learn where he was stationed. We had a record-breaking heat wave at the time and I'm sure that his presence was responsible for at least twenty degrees of it.

"Finally Bob said they were about ready to go to sea, and it was not until then that he mentioned that Lieutenant Montgomery was with them. I was perfectly furious and demanded to know why Bob hadn't brought *'the* Lieutenant' out to the house and Bob lamely said they had been too busy.

"Well, the next morning Bob left and I didn't expect to see him for a long time. I was just starting for work when the telephone rang. It was Bob. They hadn't gone and he wanted to know if I would please leave the car because he and *'the* Lieutenant' had some urgent business in town. Me, I didn't register that *'the* Lieutenant' was *'the* Lieutenant.'

"They arrived before I left and it was then I saw what

Bob had done to me. The house was in a terrible state. Lieutenant Montgomery, however, didn't appear to notice. It seems he was preoccupied with a problem of breaking out some boats. But, anyhow, he and Bob were nice enough to insist that I shouldn't go to work that morning.

"So I had to call the office and say I couldn't come down but I couldn't tell the girls that I had to stay home to entertain my husband and Lieutenant Robert Montgomery, all on account of this hush-hush 'urgent business' I had been given on the telephone. And I was dying to tell them.

"Well, the two of them sat around and tried out some polite chitchat with me and then they got down to what they really were thinking about, which was boats. After that the conversation fairly sped along and I saw that Lieutenant Montgomery was just as mad as the rest of you. It seemed that you actually intended to carry out that wild scheme of hunting submarines.

"And then, Bob, at 11:30, without warning, you said: 'How about lunch?' All the while I had expected you to dash off suddenly on 'urgent business.'

"There was no help for it. We found what we could in the refrigerator and I discovered that Lieutenant Montgomery is one of the best refrigerator prowlers in the business.

"Then Bob and 'the Lieutenant' took the car and went bouncing off to town on 'urgent business.' They came back about 1:30 with a big bag of cigarettes, gum and candy for the crew and ordered me to take them out to the boat. That was all the 'urgent business' they had.

"But anyway, I basked in reflected glory for days. It got around town, and the state, that Lieutenant (j.g.) Berry and Lieutenant Robert Montgomery were bosom pals who had fought together in the Boer War and that Lieutenant Montgomery stayed at our house for weeks.

"However, Bob, I will never forgive you for not warning me, and for all that talk about hunting submarines. I was worried to death for months. Every time I saw a paper I expected to read about those little boats floating around alone in the ocean, all because you amateur engineers got to working on them after you left port. I just knew there wasn't going to be anything to hold those boats aboard ten miles after you left the Cape."

[Lieutenant Berry smiled indulgently, administered a husbandly pat and resumed his story.]

We finally solved that problem of the PT boats. We rigged the cables holding the boats into pelican hooks secured to rings on the deck. After a few days' practice, Montgomery had his crews so trained they could man the boats and release them to float free in a minute and a half. I hate to spoil Anne's fine build-up, but we didn't really figure we could chase subs, unless, of course, our ship was actually hit. Our primary objective was to save the boats.

I think that Lieutenant Montgomery was always a little regretful that we didn't have a chance to try out the scheme, but he received other orders after the first leg of our journey, and was detached from our ship.

"I hate to stop now," he told me then. "I would like to go on and see what happens. I still think it would be an interesting experiment, getting those boats off at sea."

2

As soon as we had cleared port we resumed our gun drills in earnest. The Navy crew had drills every day, of course, regardless of where we were, and twice a week we worked with members of the merchant crew. They co-operated excellently. Conditions aboard, in fact, were very good, even though there was some bickering among the merchant sailors themselves, and a few little brushes between the two crews. The reasons for the friction, I believe, lay in the difference in ages of the men. The members of my crew were mostly boys, who felt a great enthusiasm for their jobs and the adventure in a seafaring life. The merchant sailors were older, and, to them, life at sea was a job. These men were one hundred percent patriots, otherwise many of them would not have gone to sea at all, for it was easy enough to get jobs in the war industries, but they had no illusions about what their patriotism might lead to. They yearned after comfort and the constant submarine warnings got on their nerves. I think that the youthful enthusiasm of my men just naturally irritated the older crew and this aggravated the petty difficulties that plague men who must live for months in close quarters. But, in any event, we got on splendidly. We received all the help we needed at the guns, the food was good in the beginning, and, with a group of PT crews aboard, we really had a fine time.

My gun crew was as good as first prospects indicated. Gilbert, the coxun, was about twenty-eight, well-trained, aggressive and reliable. He came from a farm down in Alabama, and his stock joke was that the Navy had to catch him to put shoes on him. He professed now not to mind them. One of our boys, Mark Ashe, a gunner's mate third class, was from North Carolina and he had been to sea plenty. He was a great storyteller and Lieutenant Bob Montgomery was one of his special auditors. We all loved to listen to his experiences, recited in a rich Carolina accent, and with such embellishment as the desired effect on his listeners seemed to require. I think it was Ashe who first told the story about the destroyer that got to sea with a quantity of green paint aboard. Ashe noticed this paint, and when he spotted a submarine surfacing about two points off the starboard bow he got out a paint gun and thoroughly sprayed the glass of the periscope. The commander of the submarine, thinking he was still looking through sea water, continued to blow his ballast tanks until the submarine rose completely out of the water and floated at an elevation of 200 feet. Then Ashe's destroyer shot it down with antiaircraft guns.

Ashe had been torpedoed just off Mombasa on the eastern coast of Africa. He was suffering from acute appendicitis pains at the time, and on the lifeboat his appendix burst.

The first mate was going to attempt an operation with a hunting knife, but then they sighted the coast and they waited until they got in. At Mombasa they found a Negro doctor who agreed to perform an emergency operation right on the dock.

The alfresco setting didn't bother Ashe, but he was worried about the doctor.

"Ah didn't know whether it was a good idea to let a cull'ed man cut up a No'th Cahlina boy," Ashe explained. "Ah figgered he might git to thinkin' 'bout my grandpappy an' he might put me together wrong, just for the fun of it. But Ah didn't have no choice, an' that doctuh did one swell job."

Once we kept books on Mark Ashe's experiences. Navy records showed him to be eighteen, but, according to our bookkeeping, he was at least forty-two.

Charbula, another of our boys, had been a dairy farmer and milkman in Texas. He had such bad eyesight he couldn't see to read a book, yet there wasn't a speck on the ocean he couldn't spot with his naked eyes—farther away than most of us could see with binoculars. His ability to spot small objects at great distances was uncanny.

The other Italian members of our crew were from Brooklyn, but they were violently loyal to the whole of New York, and when we got word at our Pacific base that the Yankees had won the series you'd have thought Hitler had committed suicide and the United States had won the war.

There were several members of the crew from Ohio and the New England states and it wasn't long before they were refighting the Civil War with North Carolina, Alabama and Texas. We fought the battle of Gettysburg all across the Pacific and back, with neither side ever gaining an inch. The razzing among the crew members was terrific at all times, but, let an outsider so much as breathe a word against any member of the crew, and the whole unit would fall on him like a ton of concrete.

Among the merchant crew my favorite was Arthur Hartung, of Brooklyn, our radio man. Sparks had been one of those "hams" who think that the universe is composed of radio waves and he was completely happy on shipboard so long as there was no radio silence, even when the food got bad. During World War I he had been a radio observer in the air force and he had once worked as an operator for the Grace Line. Sparks passionately loved his work. To him a ship was simply a contrivance for floating a wireless station. Nevertheless, he always undertook any seamanship duties connected with his job. One day an aerial insulator on the mainmast broke and Sparks would not be content unless he repaired it himself. He climbed the mast to the crow's nest. The sea was rough and the ship was rolling and one minute Sparks would be half dipped into the sea on the port side, and the next he was almost being dunked to starboard. But he sat there and repaired the insulator as if nothing was happening. Then, his job completed, he looked down. He emitted one little yelp and froze to the mast. We finally had to rig a bosun's chair to get him down.

I must tell you about Leo, the messman, whose tall tales were almost as good as those of our North Carolina gunner. Leo and Ashe used to sit together on a hatch and lie to each other by the hour.

Leo had a cat that got better treatment than the captain. Every evening Leo would walk the cat on deck, an exercise period absolutely necessary because he fed the creature so well it kept looking as though it was going to have kittens, which must have been a humiliating situation for a tomcat. Everyone aboard was very solicitious about this cat, because the story got around that if anything happened to it Leo would probably serve it up for chow. It was something to see Leo try to break the cat to lead on a line.

Leo was a wizen, unhappy-looking fellow with a big generous heart who always went out of his way to do something extra for the gun crew. He had only one vice, and that was drink, and he made a good deal of it. Just before we left port Leo came aboard very gray after a tough night on the water front. He seemed to be in need of a hair off the dog that bit him, but all he could mutter was the one word: "Hair." Leo went into the cabins of various members of the crew, and to our knowledge he drank two bottles of hair tonic, a half bottle of brilliantine, two large bottles of mouth wash, and about one-half pint of rubbing alcohol.

I came upon him the next morning, lying in the rain on

one of the hatches. I woke him up and told him to move. He said with considerable hurt dignity: "Mr. Berry, I'm a sick man."

On another of his drinking escapades Leo spent about four hours standing outside the officers' head. He swore it was a telephone booth and that he was waiting for a long-distance call from his girl friend. We put him in a hospital in New Zealand, and he made a remarkable recovery and was ready for the return trip with us. The doctor told him that if he drank again he would never recover. This frightened Leo a good bit and he was a model of circumspection all the way back. Two days after we had landed I saw Leo in New York, holding up a lamppost outside one of the water-front bars. He was talking to a friend of his up in the crow's-nest. I was very sorry for him, for Leo was a good shipmate.

3

We put out to sea in convoy, and the first night out, at about 2230 (10:30 P.M.) we underwent a submarine attack. The brazenness of a commander who would approach that close to our shores made all of us specially anxious to get a hit. The PT-boat crews were on deck, ready to attempt their launching experiment if any torpedoes started our way. We were too busy at our guns to keep an eye on Lieutenant Montgomery, but I could hear him on deck getting everything set and making jokes with the men.

The submarine commander had dared to close in on us, but he didn't attempt to surface. We stayed at our guns throughout the night. Toward morning our escorts started throwing depth charges with their Y guns, and later we heard the sound of surface fire. The action was too far away for us to see anything, but when daylight came the escort was still there and we assumed he had got the sub.

During the morning our engines broke down and we fell out of the convoy. We had just received further submarine warnings and, frankly, we were all scared. Nothing affords a U-boat a better target than a freighter that is not under way. It's like shooting fish in a barrel. My men, worn out with the vigil of the night, went back to the guns, and the PT crews resumed their stations, ready to break out their craft. This time both crews were very quiet, and, I suspect, a little jittery. Though nothing was said, you could feel a change in the temper of the men. They were aware of the odds against us if a submarine should surface then. By 1500, however, the engines were working again, and we quickly rejoined the convoy and took up our station.

Our convoy was unusually large; in fact it was organized as two units. Shortly after we resumed our position, and Lieutenant Montgomery and I had just exchanged congratulations on our good luck, two ships blew up in the midst of the lead convoy. Blinkers were going almost immediately, and at the same time General Quarters sounded. Our men were already at the guns, and in a moment our stern gun was edging about, hungrily hunting the source of the danger.

Then, right in the center of the lead convoy, a conning tower appeared. We could hardly believe our eyes, for ordinarily the sub stalks a convoy and picks off the ships on the van, known as "coffin corner." Either unusual daring or a miscalculation brought this attacker up right where we wanted him.

Ships darted in all directions, the freighters to clear the way, the escorts to get in for the kill. There was grave danger that we would shoot up each other, or that ships would collide.

The shooting started almost immediately and projectiles screeched through the air in all directions. My boys were ready to get into the fight, but we were far out of range and some of our own vessels were in our line of fire.

The destroyers closed in and shells smashed the conning tower from every angle. The men at the submarine deck gun knew they were doomed but they gamely attempted to keep firing, even when it was obvious the battle was already over. Then, abruptly, the sub went down, and the escort vessels raced across its position, dropping depth charges. There was an oil slick, and bits of flotsam, but, so far as we knew, no survivors.

The shooting that afternoon was some of the best I have seen. Every crew whose gun would bear got in a blow. I don't recall seeing more than four or five shots that missed the target. The superstructure of that sub was simply obliterated.

We didn't learn just how many men were lost from the two merchant ships that were torpedoed, but the ships sank rather slowly and help was near, so I doubt that there were many casualties.

That night we celebrated, with double watch bills.

4

We moved south and went into port, where the men practiced abandoning ship by means of nets and we had drill with lifeboats. We took aboard another Armed Guard officer, who had completed five months of gunnery courses and was coming aboard to pick up a bit of practical experience.

This dashing young junior officer was hot for action and brimful of ideas for improving the routine on our ship. He was an excellent officer, and he had a lot of ordnance theory I could not explain away. When he came to me and began telling me what we should do with the crew and the guns I was floored. For the first time since that day I thought it out on the bridge of the *Scotty* I developed buck fever and decided that Lieutenant (j.g.) Berry had no business handling guns.

Our fairly simple methods for firing our pieces seemed to serve very well for our type of gun, although I was perfectly aware that in battles of big guns at great range a more involved procedure is required. However, this complicated gunnery, which first of all requires a range keeper, didn't seem to me designed for either the men or the equipment of the Armed Guard. My crew and I had gone along on the theory that none of us knew very much, so we worked things out together and when we were done we had a way of getting hits in our practice, and a hit, they tell you in ordnance, is the final objective of naval gunnery.

But, anyway, we were not doing things right, and I, not too utterly ignorant to be unaware of my shortcomings, and with a record of no shots at a genuine sub, listened patiently to the theories, got lost in a morass of vector analysis and plotting sheets, and finally decided that we would find out what we could about advanced naval gunnery by trying it. I was determined to learn, too, if I could. After all, I had only about fifteen days training on the guns themselves. Summed up, they had told us: "This is a four-inch gun and this is a three-inch. You put a shell in here, you push this button, and it comes out there. Okay, you're a gunnery officer. Go to sea."

So we held classes on "position angle, approach angle, and aim off procedure" and prepared to enliven the port with a little practice. My gun captains and pointers listened with much interest to the preliminary lectures and then they staggered out to their gun stations and we started shooting and we couldn't hit a damned thing.

I thought that possibly the lads were just missing out of a misguided sense of loyalty to me. So we tried again, and men started running into one another and I began to be scared we'd shoot up our own boat deck.

Then the gun captains sneaked over and wanted to know: "What's all this about position angle and aim off, Mr. Berry? Damn, when you just plain shoot you can hit something. We can't do no shooting out of a book."

So we tossed theory overboard and went on shooting and I felt better, but our junior officer was very much disgusted.

Our newcomer was a bit surprised too at my method of handling the men. We had very little trouble, but once in a while a man would fail to wear a life jacket as ordered—they hated 'em—or there would be a minor case of insubordination to attend to. I handled such cases myself, believing that I best knew the men and that we ought to keep all family squabbles to ourselves. This grieved the junior officer, who had a lot of fancy notions about mast courts and general boards and the like. He also possessed a strong sense of social distinction between officers and men, whereas I had found that in the Navy any distinction is for the purposes of discipline and nothing else.

I think our junior officer was simply suffering from a case of stripe-itis and I hope he got over it. I believe he probably has, for he had the qualities of a good Navy man and needed only a little kicking around to bring them out.

Anyhow, when he left the ship, I was more than ever convinced that our rough Armed Guard methods were the best for us. I have stuck with them. I've never yet turned a man in on report, I've never had to break a man, and there

HEAVILY LADEN FREIGHTER

A heavily loaded freighter, its cargo secured above and below deck, lies in harbor prior to joining a convoy. Lieutenant Berry and his men serve on ships of this type.

HEAVY GOING

have been only four men out of all my crews who have not asked to ship over with me.

I do make the men obey the rules and regulations, in port as well as on shipboard, for I know that those rules and regulations are made for the good of the war effort, the good of the Navy, and the good of the men themselves. Particularly are rules needed in port. The men of my crews live under trying conditions, they are endlessly under strain, a strain that is only infrequently relieved by action. They are at sea months at a time and they never know when they may see a town again, so in port they are inclined to play. They are mostly wholesome kids, good American boys, and all they want is decent fun and God knows they pass up plenty of opportunities for the other kind. They'll talk on shipboard about their conquests, and about "cramming for a Wasserman" in the next port, but most of them have too much decency and too much sense to get into trouble. It is to protect the few weak ones that we enforce strict rules and I have never found that any of the men resent it. I have taken crews into many ports, some of the worst ones, but I have never yet brought back a man with a venereal disease. That I set down to the credit of the men, not to myself. I've always felt that I owe my men the right to expect of me the things I demand of them. It seems to me that there is dignity attached to the fact that I am a naval officer, and that dignity I try to uphold—it doesn't wholly preclude some occasional old-fashioned hell-raising. I demand of my men absolute cleanliness, both of their persons and their quarters, and I demand that they give the same respect to me as an officer that I give to them as enlisted men. The system seems to work. So much for Berry on Naval Leadership.

5

When we put to sea again we had one devil of a time. There were eighteen submarine alarms in six nights and most of the alerts continued throughout the night. As well as I can remember, Captain Brown and I were up without sleep from Wednesday morning until Saturday night during that portion of the trip, and the men had little more rest than we did.

At about 2130 the third night out we received a radio message that a submarine had been sighted about fifteen minutes directly ahead of our convoy. We pushed on, running by the zigzag clock, with all the men in their stations. They were all dead on their feet, but somehow, with each new alarm, you can always summon additional energy.

It was a raw, wet night, cold despite the southern latitudes, and, as I inspected the guns and watches I could fairly hear the men shivering with chill.

Just as we reached the spot where the submarine was expected, one of the ships in the middle of the convoy began to belch black smoke and her whistle blew the emergency danger signal.

Immediately there was pandemonium. Ships plowed off in every direction and there was far more danger of collision than from the submarine. The mate at the wheel cussed the

Germans, the ocean, the weather, and the merchant ships ahead and swore that the only way to safety was to ram every son-of-a-bitch who got in the way. We very nearly did, in spite of the mate's frantic efforts to avoid disaster.

Our job was to watch for subs, not to worry about station keeping. I glued to the glasses and jumped every time I saw a phosphorescent gleam on the waves.

Then the ship that had signaled sent out a blinker message saying there was a fire in the engine room and our captain called his fellow skipper a crazy, irresponsible bastard, and things calmed down a bit. We were still worried as the convoy re-formed. That lurking sub, or probably a pair of them, was about somewhere.

I went down to check the men at their stations. They were cold and wet and disgusted. I promised them hot coffee and went out in search of the steward. He couldn't be found.

I got the first mate, who had just been relieved at the wheel and was in a grim humor himself, and we quartered the deck and began hunting in earnest. Finally the mate called to me and I found him at the lifeboat station, and in the boat was the steward, hanging on for dear life. I told him what we wanted and suggested he get down to the galley and get things started. He climbed out of the boat, muttering to himself, and made off in the direction of the galley.

Twenty minutes later no coffee had appeared, so I went

below to see what could be done about getting it on deck. The galley was dark and I started another search. I found the steward in the officers' saloon. I asked him why the coffee wasn't ready.

"I don't have to make coffee at this time of night and I'm damned if I'm going to do it," he answered.

I drew my gun and fired twice. Both bullets missed him by about six inches. Then I left and in about ten minutes we had coffee and plenty of it. In fact we had coffee every night for the rest of that trip. The steward himself brought the coffee to the officers on watch. I was glad that he had seen me at pistol practice with the mate two days before. I had knocked out a dozen pop bottles without a miss, and evidently the demonstration had impressed him.

6

We arrived safely at the Canal Zone without losing a ship, although we had a total of six actual submarine attacks, somewhere along the line of the convoy, during the trip. I had always wanted to see the Canal, but the gun crew and I had been standing double watches and I was too tired to look. We went to our bunks and didn't wake up until we docked at Balboa on the Pacific side.

We were very anxious to see Panama and to investigate the mysteries of Kelly's and the Cocoanut Grove. This we did quite thoroughly and successfully. At Balboa Lieutenant Montgomery got his change of orders and we took aboard Lieutenant Hugh Robinson, USN, who was going out to command PT boats in the Pacific. He is an excellent officer and one of the finest men I have ever met. He has since been decorated for his action in the Solomons and other areas.

One night one of the PT officers and I—I do not say he was Hugh—came out of the back entrance of Kelly's. We had been having a very pleasant evening and the world was nice and rosy. There were four men outside who appeared to be Italians and they seemed to be waiting for someone and somehow or other they got the idea they were waiting for us. They jumped at us and tried to push us farther back into the dark street. What their intentions were we couldn't guess. They were very small fellows and we were right in the mood for an argument so, after a good deal of banging around, we came out of the dark side of the street with two men apiece, one under each arm. We were quite happy and proud, but then our burdens grew heavy and when we saw a policeman we went over and deposited our playfellows. Then we brushed our hands and walked haughtily away, feeling we had conducted ourselves in a manner proper for naval personnel on shore liberty. We went back into Kelly's by the front door.

The next morning I had a beautiful shiner and my friend had a hand like a boxing mitt. We heard that the Panama police had misunderstood the whole thing after our four attackers had given them an exaggerated and completely erroneous account, and the word was passed that the gendarmes were looking for two roughneck American naval officers. Our consciences were clear, but our appearance was somewhat condemning, so we stayed on board and didn't get to see any more of the country that so delighted us.

The crew, however, had a fine time. We had arranged to have them paid off when we landed and, since this was the first time most of them had been away from home, they bought everything in sight. They came aboard laden with shawls, pillows, streamers, necklaces, bracelets and similar gadgets always so dear to a sailor's heart. I almost expected to see a parrot.

7

We sailed alone from Panama and proceeded out into the Pacific, a misnomer if there ever was one. As we went south toward the Equator the weather got colder and meaner. When we crossed the Equator I wore my heavy leather gear, a pair of red woolen underwear some wag among my kinfolk had given me, and a sheep-lined coat. It all felt good.

We held Father Neptune's court for all members of the Navy personnel who had not crossed the Equator previously. That is a good ceremony on the cruise ships, but aboard our freighter, with several PT officers as special candidates, it was really something to behold. The main feature of the rites consisted of liberal application of a two-foot length of two-inch line covered with canvas and soaked in sea water. This implement of torture was wielded by a quartermaster second class and I think he weighed 210 pounds from his wrist to his elbow, because every whack raised a blister.

Each polywog was given a kind of accolade with the rope the requisite number of times, which appeared to be determined by the momentary vigor of the quartermaster second class and his personal attitude toward the candidate, and then the victim was forced to kneel before

Father Neptune, who was a chief machinist's mate decked out with a crown and a robe made from a lifeboat sail. Father Neptune conducted a severe inquisition into the social and military status of the polywog who then was forced to crawl on his hands and knees across the hatch, whereupon he was seized by several men and given a hair cut. As there were no clippers aboard, Father Neptune's helpers used a pair of sailmaker's shears and they removed the hair in bunches. Since there were a great many polywogs and the necessities of the watch called for hasty action, in some cases bits of scalp were taken out with the hair, but anything of this kind was purely accidental.

Following the haircut the polywog had his mouth washed with a mixture of salt-water soap, salt water, and engine-room oil. The purpose of this oral ablution was to cleanse away any vile words the polywog may have been uttering, or intending to utter, about this time.

The polywog was then required to crawl back across the hatch to another corner where a skull and crossbones were painted on his chest with iodine. Then a liberal application of glue was poured into his remaining hair and rope frayings were rubbed in, all part of an earnest and solemn and even solicitous effort to give him a new head of hair, as becomes a neophyte in the court. After a few more whacks with the line the ship's hose was turned on the candidate and he was well washed down with sand and canvas, applied by sturdy and willing hands. Then the polywog was patted on the back and welcomed to Father Neptune's court as a shellback.

The first of us to pass through the ordeal survived and stood around, shivering and dripping, watching with great satisfaction as the rest of the polywogs were tortured The ceremony is conducted entirely by the enlisted men of the Navy, but all officers who have not crossed the Equator are expected to go through it. None of the PT boat officers nor I had ever been south of the Equator before. There were eleven of us and you can imagine how such a prospect must have delighted the conductors of the court.

One of the officer polywogs was a rather successful lawyer from mid-Pennsylvania. As he watched and waited his turn he kept muttering to himself: "I'll never live through it. I'm going to die, I know it. This is sadistic. It's horrible!"

But he lived through it and spent the rest of the voyage in complete misery either seasick or scared to death he would be seasick.

8

During the time we were at sea we sighted neither land nor ships. The first days the sea made up, the men got sick, the navigator couldn't get a clear sky for a sight with his sextant and we didn't know where the devil we were, nor exactly where we were going. Then the Pacific calmed down and life grew so dull we hoped for a raider or a submarine to give us a little excitement.

We were well primed for any enemy who might appear. We were rather heavily armed and had the PT boats arranged so that we could discharge their outboard torpedoes, and we had a good supply of depth charges. In fact, we felt like a destroyer and we thought we could have shown a raider a good fight.

Our routine of watches and drills and cleaning and painting was well established the first days out and when the submarine menace diminished it was possible to ease the tension somewhat, and on our off hours we lay around soaking up sun and shooting the breeze.

Everyone mixed well together the first part of the cruise: gun crew, PT crews, merchant crew. It was one of the best merchant crews I have traveled with, due in good measure to Captain Brown, who knew both his ships and his men. Captain Brown himself had been in the Navy at one time, and I think he could have taken that Liberty ship to hell and back without blinking an eye. I remember the first time I saw him. He was wearing a striped suit that hadn't been pressed since he got it, a blue and white checked shirt that looked like the tablecloths in the Welland bars, green sleeve garters, a black string tie and a bowler hat. Captain Brown looks at life just as he looked to me in that outfit. He is a man I would not want to tangle with, whether he might be running a cruiser or a lumbering merchant freighter.

The mate, too, was one of those hell-to-breakfast sailing men you love to ship with, and hate to cross. He was handy with his fists, and, so he said, with the ladies. He was a little, chesty sort of man, who tried to appear dapper but somehow always succeeded in looking a little mussed. He had run on coastwise steamers and loved to tell how he had come into New Orleans or Jacksonville or Charleston at 3:00 A.M. and said to the bellboy—he knew all the bellboys as well as the night clerks, maids, telephone operators and porters—"Look me up that nice-looking blonde I had two times ago and send her up to the room and send up some ice and a couple of glasses." And then he would toss the bellboy a five-dollar bill, and pretty soon there would be the blonde—women couldn't resist him. All the bellboys, night clerks, maids and porters made a big fuss over Spike when he came to town. Best hotels in the place, too; he never stopped anywhere else.

But of course, he would add, that is all over with now.

Spike had married again, this time for keeps, and he was true. He had always been true to the women he married, believed in it. He had a son, too; hadn't seen him since the lad was four months old. Hadn't seen his wife either, and she didn't know where he was, although he called her up from all over the place every time he got into port.

I was with him one night before we left the States and Spike called his wife. He put in a call to San Francisco and immediately followed it with one to New York, and in both cases he asked his wife how she was and how the baby was doing.

Spike always went about ship announcing that he wasn't going to take anything from the goddam Navy boys—they could keep on their side of the ship and his men would keep on the other. And the first Navy boy who came messing around his men was going to get his block knocked off. So I promised Spike that if he so much as touched a Navy boy he would never know what hit him and the same went for his men. The result was, as I have said, that we all got on splendidly and the merchantmen joined us when we had church.

We all got pretty well acquainted during those long days. Our chief topic of conversation was always our jobs. We endlessly discussed ways and means of improving our work on the ship, usually winding up by discovering that the way it was done was a way dictated by long experience of better seamen than we were. Then we would grow tired of talking about ships and the sea, and the gossip would turn to the folks at home, to the ports we would see, and whether there would be any good bars or any women.

We did very little talking about what might happen to us in the war or afterward. We looked mighty hopefully to that era afterward. It seemed that every man aboard had one impelling ambition: When the war was over he was going to have a boat of his own, and he was going to sail his boat wherever he pleased, and when he got tired of sailing it he was just going to stop and get out. It seemed that everyone studied navigation sometime or other during the trip.

In the first days of our journey we figured that the World Series was on, and we had a lot of arguments with the Brooklyn contingent. But after a while we began to realize that the series was probably over, one way or another, and we couldn't keep up enthusiasm. Then we fought out the football season, and with eleven colleges and universities represented on board, the selection of the winning team and an All-American eleven took up a good bit of our time.

When talk got around to the war, it concerned chiefly what Russia was doing and the strategy we ought to use against Japan. From that we would go into the situation at home.

"I look at it this way," Montella said once. "When the war breaks out I hop right in. What chance has a guy with a name like mine got in civilian life? But, believe it or not,

I'd have gone in anyway. I'd seen enough of those letters my folks got from the Old Country. I figured my wife could get along in her job, and we didn't know then we had a kid coming. Now they both have to live on what I make and people talk about stopping inflation and already things cost twice as much as they did when the war started. When I go back I hear everybody saying what inflation will do to the farmers and white-collar workers and the laborers, but I don't hear anything about what it's already doing to wives and babies of guys who are out riding these tubs. Then there are some more strikes and everybody runs to Washington and while this goes on they want me to go out and talk to some workers about staying on the job and how production will win the war.

"Hell, they ought to know that as well as I do. I hear a lot of bitching about gasoline and sugar and coffee, but my wife doesn't say nothing except she's glad I'm back. It don't make any sense to me, all this mixup at home. I figure if we're out here shipping stuff through to guys who are getting shot up for fifty bucks a month and not grousing about overtime the people at home can go to work and keep their mouths shut. I want 'em to keep the country running in good shape so there's something to come back to when it's over."

"It ain't just strikes," said Townsend. "When Ah was back they had seven guys up for fakin' wah contracts."

"Yah, and my folks know a lawyer making sixty grand

a year getting armament contracts. The guvment needs the stuff and the company needs the work and he gets the sixty grand for letting 'em get together."

"Well, what the hell," said Townsend. "Lookit all the good experience we're getting."

"You can have the experience. What I'd like right now is a good steak and a nice cool rum collins."

"Wonder what port we'll make? They say down in Australia they close the bars at noon. Who th' hell wants a drink in the morning?"

"In Trinidad," said Townsend, "they give you drinks foh free right aftuh twelve o'clock. Can't pay foah nuthin'. . . ."

"God-awfulest hole in the world," pronounced Montella. "I got a friend down there, Sea-bee, and they're tough sons-a-bitches, but he got enough of Trinidad quick. Th' women . . ."

"They say them natives git whitah ever' day," put in Townsend.

And so it went. You could get lonesome if you let yourself, but we kept too busy to let the men think much about home. We built horseshoe games out of rope, and had a supply of darts and boxing mitts and jigsaw puzzles and magazines. The members of the gun crew painted every gun three times during the outward trip, and they were required to work at study courses that would lead them to higher ratings.

Our routine kept the men employed, and, on shipboard,

you soon begin to have the feeling that it's home and there are countless things you can find to do around your quarters, even if you rarely get to live in them. Actually, with our regular schedule of watches, drills and study courses, we kept much busier than did the merchant sailors who were navigating the ship, and, as the morale of the gun crew improved, theirs deteriorated. Toward the end of the voyage, when the food got bad, the merchant sailors were having trouble among themselves and I had to be wary to prevent fights between them and my men. Someone ought to think about shipboard recreation for the merchant crews. They deserve a better break than they get.

The PT crews didn't let the long journey worry them at all. They knew there would be excitement aplenty when they landed, and they were content to eat, sleep and play poker. The poker games went on day and night, and, since no one expected to have any use for money where he was going, the stakes looked like something from a cloakroom crap game in a state capitol. One of the men took in $3,000 in a sitting, lent part of it back to his mates so the game could continue, and then wound up broke. Everybody figured he would be sunk sooner or later with what he had anyway, so the point was to make money provide a good time any way it could.

9

It was about the twenty-sixth day out that our easy life ended and we went back to the old schedule of twenty-four hours at the guns and double watches. We were getting into enemy territory and we recruited the members of the PT crews to help on the antiaircraft guns. We stood watches in the blazing sun, the black nights, and the raw cool mornings and saw exactly nothing.

One afternoon I was on the bridge keeping an eye to proceedings and cleaning my pistol when I heard a surf breaking in the distance, and then a few minutes later I could see it, a long white line in the otherwise bright green sea. We moved on down and went through a reef and soon, as we moved up, we could see an island.

It was spring, but the island looked old and drab, with rugged, dun-colored hills running down almost to the water's edge. We moved in to the anchorage and identified ourselves to the Navy signal tower. The first question we were asked was: "Do you have any mail?" The pause in the signaling after we answered "no" seemed to say: "In such case we have no use for you." Finally the signal tower asked what our cargo was and instructed us to stand by for a pilot. When he came aboard we were presented with a problem: He spoke only French. We finally dug up a PT officer who

208

said he spoke French and after a lot of grimacing and wig-wagging he convinced the pilot that we wanted to come in, and we got under way again.

The port was as busy as I have ever seen, and was almost wholly taken over by Americans. We saw some American warships as we moved up to the dock, and our signalman asked what the place was like. The answer came back immediately: "Twenty-five percent crew liberty, hours one-five, two women, and damn little beer." At this a great groan went up and one of the PT boys said: "God, I hope we don't stay here."

I went ashore to report and found that, except for American soldiers and sailors, it was practically a ghost town. There were large stores and big, rambling homes of the type they build in the tropics, but all of the residents had gone. The windows were boarded over, the doors to the stores were locked, and on looking in you could see only bare shelves with here and there a tiny pile of dusty merchandise. I wandered across the business section and found two shops open, the Army commissary and the post office, which had in connection an ice cream and milk bar that was out of ice cream and milk. Then, on a dusty, sun-baked side street I found a small, very dirty and very crowded French bar, and discovered that all of the PT officers had somehow arrived there ahead of me. On inquiry we found they had rum, no beer, and a little cognac. The bartender, a French sailor, told us the rum tasted like a very poor grade of petrol, so we tried the cognac and decided that the petrol would have been better.

We wandered back through town, inspected a small, dusty park, which was dug full of foxholes and zig-zag slit trenches, and then I went to the American consul's office to report. He told me that most of the population had evacuated late in 1940 and early in 1941, some to Australia, some to New Zealand, and some to South America. They knew the Japs were coming.

Save for the side streets and the dust the town was really very clean and the buildings were in good repair. The few civilians I met, however, were extremely dirty and ragged and I was impressed by the immense number of dirty dogs. There were many pretty little gardens about the outskirts, but we were told by the medical authorities that because of the local practice of fertilizing the soil with human waste we were to eat no vegetables or fruits. After a month at sea it seemed mighty hard to be unable to eat some of the nice green lettuce or fresh young onions we saw in the gardens. We were told also that leprosy was quite common among the natives and that venereal diseases of all sorts were rampant.

Everywhere we went in the town we met the American Army jeep. It seems that wherever the Army goes that damn little jeep pops out at you from unsuspected corners and crannies. Coming off ship they present a greater menace than an attack by a German panzer division. There seems to be one jeep for each American soldier in foreign ports, but the Navy ashore walks. So we reverted to our college days and thumbed our way around.

At first the men were all anxious to get ashore. There was considerable squabbling in the merchant crew when they found that only one-fourth of their number could go. However, after the first liberty party had come back and reported, very few of the rest went ashore. Only six men of the Navy crew wanted to go at all. We lowered one of our lifeboats and arranged swimming and fishing parties in the bay. In between swims we would sit on deck and just look at the land. After long days at sea, land to look at is a wonderful thing, even if you aren't interested in actually stepping on it.

Meanwhile we were discharging cargo, and the merchant crew was wasting no moments. At the time it was expected that the Solomons would fall to the Japs again, and our port would be next, so there was an air of tension over the whole place. Men were busy everywhere, improving the roads, establishing gun positions and building quarters. The morale was high. The Navy was doing impossible jobs of unloading ships with little or no equipment. At the time it seemed that the work was progressing against insurmountable obstacles, but as fast as a pontoon crane tipped or broke it was righted or repaired again and those Navy engineers accomplished miracles. Almost before we knew it our PT boats were off and gone, and their crews with them.

I went aboard one of the Navy repair ships in the harbor

and after a bit of searching around found the ship's barber and got my first haircut since leaving Norfolk more than six weeks before. I positively felt lightheaded after the trimming I got.

While we were at anchor we saw several warships come in. A couple of them looked like moths had been chewing at the sides. I talked to some of the officers and they said we were being pushed around a bit, but that the Navy was doing considerable pushing around itself. They were all anxious to get stores and ammo and to get to sea again. It was a time when our fortunes of war were low. No one was sure of the future. No one spoke much of it. You could see on the face of every man you met his determination to fight like hell. We of the *Roberts* figured that we were really getting into the war.

10

Again we upped anchor and sailed alone, northward. There were no blimps or escort vessels or patrol planes now. The Navy had undertaken, as its first task, the establishment of a line of communication, established it and held it. But now we had a little job to do that was somewhat off the beaten track. There were some men up front needing supplies. We had the supplies.

We were not disturbed as we crossed those southern waters. But we kept busy. The PT crews were gone now, and we had to rely entirely on our own armament. It was good enough, we felt sure, unless a big Japanese raider got loose or we happened to run across some marauding planes. As for Japanese submarines, we didn't worry much about them. We wondered how our shooting eyes would be when we saw planes.

We were tremendously alert, and a little tense, by the time we reached our next harbor. The sea was kicking up at a good clip and we were making ten knots, intending to run in before darkness, when our forward lookout spotted a lone plane bearing 180 degrees. We couldn't tell whether it was friendly, and we couldn't take chances. We sounded battle stations and loaded our AA guns. The plane kept coming directly at us, looking more unfriendly every moment. We trained our three-inch gun on him, and I had the orders to fire in my throat when the pilot must have guessed that it was impossible for us to recognize him. All of a sudden he made a 90-degree turn and flipped his wings and I almost swallowed my field glasses in my relief. I had glimpsed our own star and thanked God I had not given the order to fire, for we had him dead in our sights.

He was a patrol plane, and he wheeled in, and we gave him the most rousing cheers I have ever heard in my life. Even Captain Brown waved his hat.

A patrol boat came out and signaled us to stand by for a pilot to come aboard. Then the signaling broke off right in the middle and the patrol boat dashed full speed astern of us. It dropped several depth charges, wheeled over the sea for a few moments, and then came leisurely back to resume the blinker conversation. A boat was lowered and came over, bringing our pilot.

The pilot told us they had picked up a strong underwater contact which they were certain was a submarine. They dropped the depth charges and then lost contact. Evidently the sub had picked up our trail and was stalking us as the patrol boat arrived. The sub had been just a few moments too late.

We proceeded into the anchorage, which was a small channel with a rather fast current. We anchored and had an opportunity to look about. This naval station was inhabited solely by a few Marines, fewer Navy men, and some head-hunters. I went ashore with the captain to report. There was no dock, so we landed on some large rocks and waded in dust up to our shoe tops to a roughly constructed shack which was the Port Director's office. The office was well ventilated with cracks big enough to fall through, and the officer's desk was two crates on which had been laid a couple of rough boards. His chair was a box, his filing cabinet a pair of boxes. That completed the furnishings of the Navy office at this port.

The Marines were busy pulling down trees and building roads and defenses for the air station. There were foxholes and slit trenches and antiaircraft guns everywhere. There had been no trouble from the Japanese yet, but the Marine officers told me that the natives were inclined to be unfriendly and that on no account should men be permitted to go into the bush alone, nor without guns ready for use.

The port was as desolate a spot as I had ever seen, and the first place I had ever visited where money, including American money, was absolutely no good. But we discovered that the Marines had pacified the natives of the nearest village enough for them to engage in barter, and I determined upon a trading expedition.

I went ashore another afternoon, while cargo was being discharged, and came across one of the native chiefs. I had been told that he was safe and that he was inclined to be a trader himself. I made signs to him indicating that I was an important American importer and he got the idea and led a couple of other officers and me to his hut behind the hills.

The chief's house was a one-room shack built of driftwood and thatched with palm leaves, but now it bore evidences of his recent contacts with civilization. He had acquired a supply of boxes, which were distributed about the shack, plugging some of the more obvious holes. In addition he was the proud possessor of several empty milk tins, a couple of pennants, a worn leather belt, and several other articles hung across the doorposts, like trophies of the chase.

We didn't go inside, but sat just outside the door and I made signs that I was ready to trade. It was very simple. I held out a cigarette, pointed to a coconut, and then pointed to my mouth. The chief, who was very old and thin and black, grinned happily, exhibiting his gums, and we traded.

I had brought along an old pair of shoes, tying the laces together and hanging them about my neck. I saw that the chief was fascinated by the shoes, so I held them out, trying to learn what he might offer for them. His old eyes sparkled, and his face wrinkled like the neck of a walrus, and he made some loud, abdominal noises and looked in at the door of his shack.

There was a stir inside, and a large, fat black woman, bedizened with shells and girded with a kind of sarong, emerged. The chief pointed to the woman, then to the shoes, then to me. I shook my head, "no," and the chief looked a little disappointed, but he made sounds again, and a second woman emerged and the chief went through his signs again.

I was feeling like an Arab trader at a slave auction, except that these women were not exactly the type you expect to see in *Esquire* and the chief was quite confounded when I again shook my head. The boys were ribbing me royally, and my gesticulations, instead of turning the chief from the subject of women, merely served to convince him that I had put a very high price on the shoes. He turned to the shack again, and a third woman emerged. She was undoubtedly the favorite, being younger and less plump, with passable limbs, firm round breasts and several teeth. The chief eyed me happily and the boys fairly rolled in the dust from laughing.

I shook my head and then got up and went over to a pile of coconuts, indicating that I would take the lot for the pair of shoes. The chief seemed a little surprised, but then he abruptly shooed his wives back into the shack, and the trading proceeded. We got a half boatload of coconuts, about three bushels of limes, and three or four bunches of wild bananas. The chief still seemed to think us a trifle addled, but he joyfully accepted the shoes. I was interested in seeing whether they would fit, but the chief didn't attempt to wear them. He hung them about his neck, imitating me, and marched proudly back to his harem.

The islands were very attractive to me. The beaches were white and clean with gently rolling hills sloping back inland, and along the shore were large areas given over to the growing of coconuts. From where we were anchored the long straight rows of trees reminded me very much of our corn fields back home. The land everywhere was green and beautiful, and the climate was ideal. The days were hot but the nights were cool. There were no mosquitoes, although during the day, when the wind died down, the flies were bad ashore. There was good fishing in the channel, and we were told that there was excellent hunting inland. Every morning, between 0830 and 0900, a big tiger shark would come into the channel. He plowed majestically about our ship, contemptuous of our guns, and then went back to sea. He repeated this ritual every day of our stay, and not once did any of the men take a shot at him. Altogether, except for the poverty and filthiness of the natives, it was one of those places you read about in the days when people were escaping life by ducking off to idyllic South Sea islands.

I had taken to sleeping at night while we were in port, and one morning about 2:30 I awoke with a jerk and sat up abruptly, banging my head against the sloping overhead. Near to us I heard a thump, and a loud explosion, and then another thump and another explosion. I leaped to the deck and charged up the ladder.

We were being shelled from seaward, and some shelling it was. You could easily see the big projectiles flash through the night. They seemed to hover over us, and then to drop abruptly, too close for comfort.

We couldn't see what was shelling us and we were told

LIEUTENANT (j.g.) CRAIG HOWRY AND LIEUTENANT BOB BERRY
This picture was taken at a sidewalk café in Africa.

LIEUTENANT BOB BERRY'S GUN CREW FOLLOWING THE BATTLE OF SICILY

not to leave our anchorage. Then the enemy appeared to get his range, and the shells began dropping onto the beach, and back among the hills where the airfield was being constructed. The shelling continued for a half hour and destroyers were dashing out all through the attack, and then there was more shelling and everything was quiet. There was no damage to us, save for the loss of sleep and general wear and tear on our nerves.

The next morning we could find no one who would admit knowing what had happened. It wasn't until that night that we learned about our visitor when we picked up a broadcast saying we had been shelled by an unidentified enemy warship.

In time—quick time, considering the difficulties—we discharged most of our cargo and were prepared to move off for the next stop. Then word came through that one of the Japanese aircraft carriers had eluded our fleet and was supposed to be heading in our direction.

This news worried Captain Brown, who had been all for going after the enemy shelling us a few nights before. He didn't mind the carrier and her planes so much, but he didn't want to run through our own mine fields at night. He said that if he was ordered to do it he would have pups right on the bridge.

But ships had to go out, carrier or no carrier, and one of the big transports was selected to try it. That night, a short distance off shore, we heard an enormous boom, and a huge glare lighted the sky to seaward. The harbor quickly became live with boats, and then things quieted down again, as suddenly as they had started. We decided that a submarine had caught the transport as it maneuvered out of the mine field, and we hoped that the men were saved.

The next morning the channel was filled with oil, life jackets, life rafts and floating debris. From the extent of the wreckage we decided that there had been a terrible catastrophe. However, we later learned that only four men had been lost, although this was bad enough, for food was short on the island and there was no shelter for the men who had been put ashore. Everyone in the harbor shared food, sailcloth and blankets with the survivors, but there wasn't enough and many of the men, badly shaken by their experience, had to sleep on the ground without blankets, and the nights were cold. I don't know how the problem was solved, for the next day we shoved off. The Navy had located the carrier and was giving her a merry time.

It was in those waters that we narrowly missed a bombing attack. We were alongside jungle country, and the fighting was mean; about thirty raiders came over, too high for the guns. They were after a group of destroyers, they were not interested in merchant ships, and not many of them came back to repent of that mistake.

Our only contact with the men doing the big share of the fighting in those parts was when we dropped anchor in an obscure cove and groups of Marines dashed out to us in little native canoes, loaded with bananas. The Marines were yelping like Indians, demanding to know whether we had any mail, and when we didn't they wanted to trade the bananas for gum and candy. We scraped together everything we could find on board, and traded. It was really an amazing sight—those tough, tanned young banana merchants whooping it up in their makeshift bumboats, going into frenzies of delight because they had run into a little supply of chocolate bars and chewing gum. Some of these lads, we discovered later, were among a group of Marines sent out to rid a tiny island of 350 Japanese reported to have installed themselves there. The Marines went into the island in the morning, and came back that night, bringing evidence that 348 of those Japs were no longer alive and kicking. The boys were cussing because they figured someone had given them a wrong count on the enemy they were to meet. They couldn't find the other two. They are playing for keeps out there in the Pacific, and the men I have seen there are men who know how to handle themselves.

11

We made south, and in due time saw the cool, green hills of New Zealand.

There we got a royal welcome. The harbor was a hectic bustle of activity, with American ships unloading and American engineers building docks and barracks, and American troops streaming ashore at all hours of the day and night. The New Zealanders were absolutely amazed at the speed and efficiency of the Americans; they could talk of nothing else.

The town itself seemed like home. In the first place it was jammed with American sailors, Marines and soldiers, but actually it was the people of New Zealand who made us feel we were back in the United States. We were received with great friendliness everywhere, and it was not at all unusual for an American sailor on the street to be approached by some elderly man, dressed in typical English bowler, striped pants, black coat and wing collar, who invited him to tea. The first time I was approached I thought I was meeting Chamberlain. I have always heard a lot about British reserve, and I have heard that the New Zealanders are more British than the British themselves. If that is true, it speaks mighty well for English hospitality, for never before in my life have I been received more graciously and enthusiastically than in those New Zealand homes.

Downtown, in the stores, there was an equally keen enthusiasm for Americans, and in my opinion the stores and shops provide the true test of a city's hospitality. New Zealand had rationing, and we of course had no ration books. The merchants got us supplies nevertheless, taking their chances with the rules, and it wasn't a black market. They felt they would be able to explain the circumstances to the officials and they took a chance. The prices they charged were reasonable. The New Zealanders quite frankly admitted that since their troops were in the Middle East they would be quite defenseless if it wasn't for the Americans. They were grateful, and they showed it.

I was struck by the complete absence of young men in the town. Down at the docks, where in any American city you would see scores of husky youngsters, there were only older men and cripples. Those New Zealand stevedores couldn't work fast, but they worked steadily and they did a good job.

Already the Americans had made an impress on the people and habits of New Zealand. Prior to the arrival of our troops there were no Sunday movies, no restaurants or tobacco shops open after 6:00 P.M., no ice-cream bars nor hamburger stands in the whole city. But shortly before we visited the port the blue laws were lifted, an enterprising merchant opened a hamburger shop, several ice-cream cafés were started, and everything remained open long past sundown. The places were jammed, not only by Americans but by New Zealanders, who seemed to get a bigger kick out of it all than we did. I went to a Sunday movie, my first in months. Abbott and Costello were playing, and a Western feature (yes, they even had the double feature!) and the crowd whooped it up. It was no tea-and-crumpets crowd, but one typically American, although at least half those present were New Zealanders. We really felt at home.

The stores in the port were well stocked with merchandise, and the restaurants amazed me: I wrestled with some of the biggest steaks it has ever been my pleasure to meet. The coffee, however, was atrocious, almost as bad as that I got later on a British battleship while messing into the Atlantic side of the war. I suppose that the amazing thing is that I got coffee at all, at either place. The only public criticism I heard of Americans concerned our table manners. Our New Zealand friends were a little astonished that we used a fork with the wrong hand. However, one host confided to me that he had always believed Americans ate entirely with their knives, and he professed to be agreeably surprised to learn that this was untrue. The mild New Zealand horror of persons who do not employ the fork sinistrally astonished me a little. On numerous occasions kindly hosts tended my every want with great solicitude, and refrained from any utterance that possibly could be interpreted as critical, only to blurt out finally: "Lieutenant, why is it Americans do not use the fork in the left hand?"

By night the town was very dark, for blackout orders were strictly enforced. I talked with several policemen, grand fellows—somehow I always like policemen—and they told me that crime in New Zealand has decreased markedly since the blackouts. I was chatting one night with a pair of officers when a crowd of American soldiers spilled into the street and a great free-for-all started. Several other New Zealand policemen came up, and they all watched delightedly, shouting their pleasure and approval when a particularly good punch was landed. Finally the Army MPs broke up the fuss and I heard one New Zealand policeman say: "That was a jolly good go, wasn't it? Such vigor!"

New Zealand traffic bothered me a good deal, and I am a veteran from traffic bouts in such places as Boston, South Bend and Sioux Falls. Cars kept to the left of course, and it seemed they were always popping out at us with diabolical intent. I was in greater danger ashore than on the submarine lanes, and I know I ruined the nerves of a good many New Zealand truck drivers who narrowly missed clipping me. I finally learned to get about by looking carefully both ways and then dashing madly for the other side of the street. I took no chances. My salvation was that automobile prices are so high in New Zealand there are few of them.

There was a war on, unquestionably, but it didn't much disturb the New Zealand businessmen. I saw a sign in one of the leading jewelry store windows which seemed to typify the New Zealand attitude. It read: "We beg to intimate to our friends and patrons that this establishment will be closed all day Saturdays." Life for the New Zealand man of commerce seems to be an endless business holiday. There were morning holidays, midday holidays, afternoon holidays, and all-day holidays. It seemed that every time I wanted to buy something the store was closed because of a holiday.

New Zealanders, I found, have long memories and boundless gratitude. Several of us hired a cab for a sight-seeing trip, and the driver, a little, bright-eyed, whiskery man, gave us a stated price for a two-hour tour. Then he drove us everywhere in his 1912 Dodge. We were delighted for the first two hours, but then we grew weary. Our driver, however, had become really interested in his city, and he kept repeating that he had never before seen some of the spots we visited. We finished the usual routine of shrines and parks and museums, and went on to conservatories, cricket fields and major industrial establishments. Our driver even attempted to get us into the government house, but it was closed. Holiday. We were out more than four hours, but the driver refused to take any more than the two-hour price, because, he insisted, he had as much fun as we did.

"I wuz in Newport News in th' last war," he told us. "Th' populace there wuz very good to us. I said then, I said, sometime I will git even. Well, now, buddies, this is th' time."

Our greatest disappointment in New Zealand was at the

bars. There was lots of warm beer, and a vile drink called shandy, which seems to consist of lemonade and beer. Shandy is quite popular, but I don't know how they do it. There was a desperate shortage of Scotch and no bourbon nor rye. In fact, each bar is given four bottles of Scotch a day, which they promptly sell out when they open at 10:00 A.M. It is very inconvenient to do one's drinking at that time of the morning, but Americans are very pliable people, and all of us managed to suit our customs to those of our hosts.

The barmaids, waitresses and sales girls are all madly in love with American soldiers and sailors and are carefully saving their money so that they may go to the United States after the war. If they go to the Midwest they'll be right at home, for any one of them might have come from Indiana or Kansas.

Even the women of uncertain reputation—and there were not many of them—were utterly fascinated by the American uniforms. I remember one night shortly after we had arrived in port the merchant crew had been paid off and their pockets were bulging with rolls of bills and they were out for a good time. Two of them picked up two young women and started out with the announced intention of seeing how quickly good American money could be exchanged and spent.

The merchantmen took the girls to their hotel for drinks as the preliminary to a large evening, and in the lobby they met two boys from the Armed Guard. The merchantmen, confident of their financial prowess if not their own charms, generously introduced the girls.

"Listen, baby," spoke up one of the Guards promptly, "we don't have any money so we can't spend any, but look at our uniforms! Why don't you gals go with us?"

So the young ladies uncermoniously ditched their wealthy escorts and went off with the pair of uniforms.

12

We moved on about the island, through beautiful fjords cutting deep into mountains that I am told resemble the Alps with a bit of ocean dropped in, and finally came to anchor in a quiet little inlet that seemed thousands of miles away from war and turmoil. It was not many hours before the people learned that Americans had arrived, and we were deluged with enough invitations to dinners, parties and dances to keep us busy for months. Our next call was at Dunedin, which looks and acts like an American city, even to the extent of carrying sheer exuberance and boisterousness into the twilight zone of lawlessness. What impressed us most at first were the Dunedin bars, each secluded in a side street, and entered only after the customer has been peered at through a tiny window in the door. It reminded me of Chicago in Prohibition days. Why the bars should be so secluded none of us could understand, for quite obviously they were no secret to the Dunedin natives and it seemed that in them we met everyone in town.

Dunedin hospitality outdid anything I had previously known, and it's my personal opinion that the town ought to crowd Chicago's reputation as a host to servicemen. We were invited everywhere, and the enthusiasm for Americans was so honest, and openhanded, and at times downright violent that we felt like Hollywood stars on a personal appearance tour.

To me, the happiest part of the Dunedin experience was my meeting with Father Harrington. It happened quite by accident. One of the men of the crew saw Father Harrington on the street and decided that he was an exact double for me. He insisted that we should meet, and the good Father was glad to comply. I am told, and I believe it and am very proud of it, that the resemblance between us is amazing. Father Harrington and I met, shook hands, commiserated with each other on our mutual misfortune, and immediately became good friends.

Father Harrington was born in Cork, and he had come to New Zealand directly after taking his orders. I cannot guess his age. He seemed very young, but he had the poise and quiet strength of a man old and wise in the ways of life.

He invited several of us to be his guests, and we climbed aboard his old Ford and rattled out into the country, some of the loveliest country in the world, green and cool and peaceful. Father Harrington had two small parishes, situated about thirty miles from Dunedin, and we went with him as he made his calls.

The people were like the farmers at home in South Dakota. They were very glad to see us, in the quiet, serene way of farmers well content with their lot, and the sight of Father Harrington's car spurting up the country lane immediately sent the womenfolk into the kitchens. We consumed gallons and gallons of tea, untold numbers of cakes and sandwiches, and much more Scotch than was proper. We were taken on tours of the farms and learned that New Zealanders have a funny habit of putting blankets on their cows. I guess it's as good sense as blanketing horses.

Everywhere we went the people wanted to know about America. Was our country as big and strong and resourceful and generous as they had heard? How quickly would the Americans whip the Japanese? Would America take over New Zealand as a colony? That latter question was on everyone's lips, farmers, bankers, businessmen, sailing men, housewives. I gained the impression that New Zealanders believe their future is henceforth bound very closely to that of the United States. They feel that we are very good friends, and I am sure that they are very good friends for us to have.

Sunday we went to Father Harrington's Mass, in a pretty little country church set like a tiny white gem among the New Zealand hills. He dedicated this Mass to the American Navy.

"The people of New Zealand," he said, "owe a great debt to the people of America. We especially owe a great debt to the men from that fine republic who are now in service on New Zealand soil, and who are fighting the battle of a free people in every part of the world. May God bless them, and people of righteousness everywhere, and our own sons far from home!"

The service was beautiful and our throats were tight with emotion when it had concluded. Then we met more people, quiet-spoken, clear-eyed people who had found in the friendly soil of New Zealand those freedoms their sons were now defending in far-off Egypt and England. It was another experience I shall never forget.

That afternoon we went on another tour with Father Harrington. We had so many invitations to dinner and tea that I began to fear for my health, even though New Zealand meals are unusually good and are prepared much in the fashion of those at home. The people of the community pooled all their available gasoline and gave us a car and driver so that we might visit as many homes as possible.

There was one special stop on our list—the O'Hallorans, west of town. They had just received news that two of their sons in the Royal Air Force had been killed on raids over Germany. They had written Father Harrington to ask that we come to see them.

Their cottage was tiny and white and exceedingly well kept, like all the farm homes in that part of the country, and the yards and grounds were as trim as those you might expect on an English country estate. In the pasture near the house grazed a fine herd of cattle—we had already eaten some of Mrs. O'Halloran's splendid butter at Father Harrington's.

Mr. O'Halloran, strong, ruddy, graying just a bit at the temples, met us in the yard as we drove up. He wrung our hands with the strength of a man whose emotion is great, but whose sense of the eventual justice of God is even greater. He even smiled a little as he welcomed us. It was not until Father Harrington placed a kindly hand on his shoulder that he seemed broken for a brief moment, but then he drew himself up, tossed off any momentary weakness and asked us to come into his home.

Mrs. O'Halloran was exactly as we expected, a plump, kind-eyed Irish lady starch-aproned and pink from her work in the kitchen. "Bless you, you've come!" she cried to us. And we giggled like schoolboys when she threw her arms about us and made us welcome.

We talked about home, the places we had seen, of our love for New Zealand, and about the O'Halloran boys.

"Jamie wrote us when he was in New York," Mr. O'Halloran said. "The people there were very good to him, very good. You cannot realize, Lieutenant, how much knowing that means to us now. Jamie was our youngest."

Then Mr. O'Halloran broke out his best bottle of Scotch and we drank with him, toasting the RAF and New Zealand, and the Army and Navy of the United States.

"Lieutenant," said Mr. O'Halloran with great sincerity, "if I were a younger man, just ten years younger, I would sell everything after the war and go to America to live."

Mrs. O'Halloran smiled at us and at him, and her eyes, gently sad, wandered about the room and she looked absently into the stairway and then out toward the yard and barn and we knew that her thoughts were with the two lads who had grown to manhood in that house and had tended the cattle and plowed the quiet fields and then had gone off to war.

13

While we were in Dunedin other ships came in, and Father Harrington began a self-appointed mission: to meet every foreign ship and to go aboard and talk with the men, to conduct a Catholic service for those who desired it, and to offer to write home for any men who wished him to do so. I hope that he may never miss a ship. He brings something great and good, something men know they need after a tussle with the sea. Also he brings a friendliness that is warm as the sun and fresh and stimulating as the winds that cool the New Zealand fjords.

To the men who may welcome him, I have one suggestion: Be sure to invite Father Harrington to the mess for coffee. He won't admit it, but he loves it. Gallons of it. In his parish Father Harrington drinks tea, but on an American ship with a five-inch gun Father Harrington has learned the delights of good, strong, black American coffee and I earnestly hope that his refusal of just another cup will be rejected gently, but with firmness.

14

When we left New Zealand all of the men not assigned to duties were on the stern, waving to the crowd on the docks. Some of the boys were actually blinking back tears, or, at any rate, so it seemed. One turned to me. "Gee, Mr. Berry," he said, "do you think we'll ever get to come back here again? I left a swell girl behind."

We pushed out into the Pacific, below the lanes of submarines and raiders, and we had a genuine opportunity to enjoy travel by sea. It was an uneventful voyage, calling at two South American ports, the two most contrasting ports a sailing man might ever expect to find.

The first was downright dirty, the people were ragged and undernourished and very unfriendly, and the Nazi spies were doing a great business.

Oddly, it was in this town that we got the best food we had found on the trip, save for our first port in New Zealand. Enormous steaks were obtainable in every restaurant, and there seemed to be a plentiful supply of everything. In the cafés and hotels the people appeared to favor the Allies in the war, and we received some friendly gestures because we were Americans, but down at the docks, and among the stevedores and poorer people, we found only enmity, which may have been hatred of Americans in particular, or just foreigners in general. I was unable to discover its exact extent or the reason for it.

The natives had experienced some previous contact with English-speaking persons, we discovered, and had picked up some English words, notably "bastard" and "bitch," which they used to describe everything and everyone, good or bad.

Montella, from our gun crew, seemed the only one of us able to get along well with the men around the docks. One evening I saw him coming toward the ship with his arm about the shoulders of one of the dock workers. As they parted, Montella was patting his friend on the back, saying with a big friendly grin: "Good-by now, you dirty bastard, you son-of-a-bitch, you low-down good-for-nothing dirty yellow dog." The dock worker thought he was being highly praised and he was beaming and shaking hands with Montella and saying loudly: "*Sí, sí, señor! Adiós. Adiós. Buenas noches, mi amigo.*"

One night, shortly after midnight, I heard a big noise on deck and went out to investigate. There was a mob just off the gangplank and the men were cursing in Spanish, Portuguese, French and several other languages and threatening to storm the ship. Coxun Gilbert was standing guard and I knew that he was not a man to get into trouble so I couldn't imagine what had happened.

I questioned Gilbert and learned that some of the dock workers had attempted to force their way aboard without passes. That was strictly against the rules and Gilbert, who had a gun, had refused to let the men on deck. They first attempted to rush him, but when Gilbert was determined, they contented themselves by heckling him and attempting to whip up enough courage for violence.

I attempted to talk with them, to find out what they wanted, but I couldn't make myself understood. More men collected in the mob, and leaders were haranguing them and things began to look serious.

I called out the gun crew and ordered all the guns trained on the crowd. It dispersed in a hurry.

Gilbert was very happy at this, and he kept repeating to me: "By Heaven, Mr. Berry, they ain't got passes and I wouldn't let anybody aboard without a pass, not even the President."

Soon the mob returned, and this time it was led by some kind of local official. He marched up importantly and delivered a tirade in a language I couldn't understand. I didn't want any trouble, so I picked up a rifle and aimed directly at the official and then announced in English that everyone had better get the hell out of there. The official vanished ahead of everyone else and again the mob dispersed. They didn't know there was no ammunition in the rifle.

After a while we learned the reason for the trouble. The men had been accustomed to come aboard the ships they were loading about midnight for hot water for their tea. Passes were required of course. This night the local officials had failed to distribute the passes, and the men on the loading rafts expected to get aboard without them.

We finally got the thing settled. The men got their passes and their tea, and we were out no more than a night's sleep.

We did not spend much time in the town, and I was rather glad that the people were so unfriendly as to keep the men on the boat. For the red-light area extended into the heart of the business district, and representatives of the various inmates were on every corner, in the persons of little bootblacks, nine or ten years old. After shining your shoes the urchins would hand you a printed advertisement for one of the houses, urging: "You see Marie, mister. She nice. She only go with American officer. She my sister."

The second port was clean and friendly and wherever we went we heard *vivas* and cheers for the Americans. Why there should be such a startling contrast in two cities but few miles apart I cannot guess, but we quickly revised our opinion of the people and the country. We had only two days in that port but they were enough to cause me to share the enthusiasm of friends who are determined to go to South America to live when the war is over.

We narrowly averted an international incident, however, despite the warm friendliness of the port. As we put to sea again, and had left the coast well behind, we resumed our double watches because of a report that a German raider was in the vicinity. The raider was supposed to be a destroyer-type craft, partially camouflaged as a merchantman.

The night was very dark, and shortly after midnight the watch reported an object sighted to port and coming up fast. We manned the guns and waited. It looked like a destroyer. It was hell to wait, but we held our fire, and finally the strange ship signaled. We answered with the name of our vessel and expected to get a projectile for our care.

There was a tense moment of waiting, and then the stranger blinked something we couldn't understand and we repeated our name again. A searchlight went on aboard the stranger, and we were ready for trouble. Then the light swung up and rested on the truck of the mainmast, disclosing a neutral flag. It was a South American patrol boat and we were glad all over the place. One shot that night would have landed us in a peck of trouble.

15

We spent Christmas at sea. I had gone shopping in the last port and had a store of candy aboard for the men. The steward had gone shopping, too, with funds of the merchant sailors, but he had been distracted from his purpose and had come back with two black eyes and no supplies nor money. So all of us had Christmas together. The boys gave me a present, one I spent half the afternoon unwrapping. Inside the bundle of paper I found a matchbox containing two Norfolk car tokens. I was glad to get them. I was hoping to use them soon.

Our voyage up the South American coast was mean. The weather was cold, the sea was rough, and the ship rolled 30 degrees day after day. We slept again through the canal, and did not experience another submarine attack until we were almost home.

The night was very dark and the wind was like a blast out of Labrador. The ship was rolling and the waves were lashing the decks as we stood to battle stations, and one of the gunners, homesick at last after six months away, was sobbing at his gun. He pretended he was sniffling from a cold as I came up and he demanded angrily: "Hell, Mr. Berry, why did it have to happen here? If we're gonna be hit why couldn't it happen down where the water was nice and warm instead of here in this damn ice and cold?"

We didn't get hit, nor did we see the submarine. We had traveled 25,000 miles and we hadn't had a shot at anything.

I was anxious to be home. I hadn't heard from Anne since we left, and I was worried. The baby was expected New Year's Day, or thereabouts, and I had been plagued for weeks with all sorts of fantastic ideas about what might happen.

We were almost in port when a heavy fog hit us. Our horn was going as we pushed through the night, and we had a double watch on duty. We entered the harbor, where the shipping was heavy, and reduced our speed. Sailing through heavy fog with a darkened ship in a dimmed-out port is no picnic.

Then it happened. The most inglorious, ridiculous, tragic thing that could possibly happen to any ship just returning from a 25,000 mile cruise to the war.

We were a half hour from the dock. Out of the fog a freighter wallowed across our bow. Fogs are sometimes tricky—they toss the sound about until your horn is absolutely meaningless, and it is never possible to know whether or not it is guiding you accurately. Visibility was zero. We crashed, a heavy, dull, earth-shaking thud.

Men were thrown about the ship and no one had the slightest idea of what had happened. But Captain Brown was on the job. He kept his engines going ahead. To reverse the engines at such a time, which would seem the normal reaction, would merely pull your ship's bow out of the hole made by the collision and permit the water to rush in before the crew of the other ship could shore up her bulkheads.

It became obvious in a moment that both ships would remain afloat. Tugs came out to take charge of the other freighter, and we made our way slowly into port. We were taking water rapidly, but the pumps were able to stand against it, and we finally warped to the dock. The other ship, I learned later, had to be beached.

Safe ashore, I raced to the first telephone. Anne had gone to Pittsburgh to have the baby, I knew, for we had planned that before I left. I got the home of her parents and, without learning who was answering the telephone, demanded:

"How's Anne? Has the baby come?"

There was a dead silence. Finally the voice asked: "Bob Berry? You?"

"Sure it's me! How's Anne?"

"Thank God!" said the voice, that of Anne's aunt. "Anne is all right. You're a father. You have a little son, born one hour ago!"

I got to Anne Monday. It was not until then I learned my ship unofficially had been considered missing for weeks. We had gone too far off the beaten track down under, and somehow went unreported when we did make port. Poor Anne! She had a bad time of it. It seems that I can remember everything that happened on that trip, but I still can't remember what happened between the time I called Anne in Pittsburgh on Saturday afternoon and the time I saw her Monday morning.

Part III

INVASION

1

IN MY opinion the Armed Guard is a good duty. You travel over the world, an attraction of the service that almost daily expands and increases, you have liberty in strange ports, when you sleep in your bunk you sleep warm and dry, you enjoy shipboard cleanliness and comfort and generally you eat very well indeed. I think that I will never join the school of Melville's skipper who swore that he had taken his last dose of salts and would forsake the sea forever. I still want my own boat when this show is over. But yet, after almost six months of the Pacific in one gulp, I was not too unhappy that day in February when I received orders for a brief tour of duty ashore.

Several of us who had gained experience at sea were selected as instructors in the expanding Armed Guard educational program. During those first months of the war our outfit, it appeared, had won a reputation. In the beginning, masters and owners alike had not been too sure that they wanted guns and a gun crew aboard, but experience had demonstrated that we were really worth while. We had kept the subs and the planes away from the bulk of our seaborne commerce, protecting the men and the ships delivering the goods. We didn't shoot often, but when we did it was to good account. Somehow, during that first fifteen months of the war the Battle of the Oceans had been fought and won, and the Armed Guard had its part in the victory. Now they wanted us, and hundreds of new ships were coming off the ways, and the demand for gunners was great. So we who had been to sea turned to teaching and for our reward were promised that when offensive action started we would get into the thick of it. All of us in the Guard by then had our own personal reasons for desiring a good shot at the enemy. Of the ten of us who had started at Little Creek, for example, five had been lost in action and most of the rest had been sunk at least once. We felt, all of us who were left, that we had earned the right to a crack at them, and the commandant at the Center made it clear that such an opportunity was exactly what we were going to get. But first the teaching chores had to be completed. We, as men of experience, were to apply the finishing touches to a training program that made our initial schooling at the Creek look like kindergarten stuff.

We promptly got out and met our classes, around some fine new guns. Our pupils, we discovered, were not the utter greenhorns we had been. They had had two months of navigation, seamanship and ordnance at Dartmouth or Princeton and another month of practical AG work at Boston or Little Creek before coming to us. Those three months of training made all the difference in the world. We were getting men who had been no nearer the sea than Customs tower in Boston, yet who knew all about communications,

PETTY OFFICERS OF LIEUTENANT BERRY'S GUN CREW IN THE SICILY ENGAGEMENT

A GUN-CREW MEMBER RIGS SPECIAL CONVOY LIGHTS

The convoy lights of Lieutenant Berry's ship were shot down during the Battle of Sicily.

taking boats through the surf, bore-sighting a five-inch gun, getting a line to a stranded vessel, or figuring a torpedo course on a chartroom mooring board. Believe it or not, they really knew those things and they were ready and eager to be practical about them.

The crews also came to us well prepared for the work that lay ahead of them. They had been with their officers in the training at Boston or the Creek and they had received the same kind of instruction.

Those lads, to whom we were to bequeath the benefits of our long experience at sea, really knew more about some phases of the job than we did, and I, for one, was wishing I could have shipped out again immediately, rather than face them.

But there are always a few little wrinkles you can acquire here and there during the course of a long cruise and we were challenged by the type of officers and men we were getting. Too, we had the prestige sea duty gives one. Any man ashore in the Navy seems to worship those who have been riding the blue. We got that kind of adulation, and we made the most of it.

The new Merchant Marine crews given into our training care were of the same stamp as the Naval Reserve officers and men. Most of the members of these crews had chucked better jobs in their own calling to follow the sea. They were alert, aggressive and industrious, and they learned rapidly.

The most fun in our work was the training-ship course,

which now, as in the beginning, is the most important part of the Armed Guard curriculum. You go to sea with your neophyte officers and men and work out your problems practically, hashing them over by night in bull sessions called seminars. No graduate seminar ever operated like those aboard the AG training ships. The instructor dared not call for questions for if he did he'd talk all night.

I guess that the reputation of the American Armed Guard had become international, for during the late part of my shore duty I was ordered to report on a ship out of Murmansk bearing an unpronounceable Russian name. I thought at first that she was a Liberty honoring our ally, but when I got aboard I saw that she was one-hundred-percent Russian and I almost dropped in my tracks when they presented the members of the gun crew. They were all women.

Those Russian girls dressed like men, looked like men, acted like men, and they really handled the guns. I gave the instructions in English, and an interpreter translated. The women were quick to learn and they carried out orders almost without flaw. In a couple of days they had even picked up a bit of English. I, in turn, learned Russian. *Awchen horoshia pagoda*—It's a beautiful day. *Yah droog* —I am a friend. *Zdra' stvouitje*—How are you? *Kakoy ehtot gorud.* . . . I am afraid to put all of the phrases in print, for I remember Montella and his stevedore friend in South America. However, I think the Russian girls were too earnestly concerned with the war to play any pranks on their American instructor.

Teaching the Brazilian crew was a little more difficult. One of our boys knew English and Spanish, and one member of the Brazilian crew knew Spanish and Portuguese. So eventually the instructions got across in Portuguese and the right things seemed to happen to the guns. But I was never too sure about our line of communications.

2

Things were cooking while we were busy with our pedagogical tasks, and the odors therefrom were particularly noticeable around the Navy's scuttlebutt. Gossip and rumor were rife, and, while Navy scuttlebutt is about eighty-five percent inaccurate most of the time, we began to have the idea that we would be shoving soon, and for something more than shooing subs and planes from well-laden transports.

My first official intimation that I would have a new part in the war came in the wake of a heavy wash of rumor, but it still caught me quite unprepared for the magnitude of my opportunity. I received my orders and reported to my ship. What a ship! She was everything an Armed Guard officer could dream of. A big, bosomy transport, loaded with guns until she looked like an overturned centipede. I was as happy as any AG officer could ever ask to be. We had shooting irons to put us up in the warship class. Perhaps that is a bit of exaggeration, but, anyhow, the *Bouncing Betsy's* armament outclassed the old *Scotty* as the *South Dakota* surpasses a destroyer. I knew then, and very surely, that we were going out to get something. I was confident that all the scuttlebutt concerning the Armed Guard's part in a coming offensive was going to prove true.

But still, my first two cruises on the *Betsy* were tame enough. We crossed the Atlantic with only the usual submarine alarms; we pushed into the Mediterranean sighting only a few distant planes; we loaded wounded and prisoners and brought them to the United States. It was our wounded who applied the soubriquet *Bouncing Betsy* to our ship, and, in case any Axis agents are listening, that affectionate cognomen has no connection with her real name. But how it fits! The *Betsy* had been on a coastwise honeymoon run and had been converted. In placid waters she rode beautifully, but out from shore she danced around like a frisky broncho. The binnacle list for the crew looked like a roll call at a Service Men's Center. The *Bouncing Betsy* rolled and pitched and yawed and sagged and hogged, but she kept right on going through the black waters, much to the disgust of many young soldiers who were praying for an early sinking so they could get out to look for their stomachs.

Our wounded on those trips were a splendid bunch of men. They cursed the *Betsy* with everything they had, but they could really take it and they wound up loving her, for, after all, the *Betsy* was taking them safely home. I particularly remember one young flier. He had cracked up in Africa and was found unfit for further duty. When he boarded our ship his hands shook so he couldn't hold a cup of coffee. But he developed a fondness for the *Betsy,* and poked into her holds and decks until one of the doctors, observing his interest, got him into the wheelhouse to try his hand at navigation. It was not long before our young aviator was taking sun sights and plotting courses, and before we reached home he was apparently cured and raring to get back into action again.

The *Betsy* interested our Nazi prisoners too. In the beginning they simply refused to believe she existed. They had been told that the United States possessed no armament, and when they saw ours they said it was all a fake. Then we did some shooting, and the prisoners said that we were a special ship, sent out for the express purpose of fooling them. The Nazis also had been told that New York was bombed to the ground. They refused to believe anything was left of Manhattan until we steamed into the harbor and they were convinced. After all, it is mighty hard to deny New York.

Those Nazis, incidentally, were some of the best from Hitler's legions. They were fit and well trained and they maintained excellent discipline all the way across. The American Army major in charge of them nearly exploded one day when he went down for inspection and the Germans solemnly lined up and heiled Hitler for his benefit. But, after they saw New York, their starch was gone. They knew then, at last, that they had been lied to from A to Zygo by the Nazi propaganda ministry. New York was simply too much for them.

3

But it wasn't my intention to talk about those first cruises. They were simply run-of-the-convoy junkets to Africa and back and nothing happened, except that occasionally we were scared to death and our escorts dropped some depth bombs and we saw some oil slicks that looked very good.

The third trip, for that matter, began like all the rest. They had been moving trainloads of men and equipment coastward for weeks and perhaps months but we never guessed that the real thing was coming up. In truth, we didn't suspect it until H hour itself arrived. So far as we knew, this trip was to be no different from the rest. Procedure was the same. Our passengers were the same.

We had a goodly number of them—noisy, happy, sun-tanned lads who had put in long months at the training camps and who were chafing for the opportunity to prove to the world they could outfight any German. Our boys were fresh from camp, fit, hard, well trained. They didn't know it then, and neither did we, but their endless maneuvers in the States were no war games for exercise. There were to be but few finishing touches in foreign training fields. We were on our way to a scrap.

Things were no different as we loaded that night at an east-coast port. The troops had been moved secretly, as usual, and all the customary precautions had been taken for security. Things were so secret, in fact, that it is quite remarkable any of us made our ships. We thought we were bound for Africa. We would shuttle back within a month, of course. Not even the scuttlebutt had caught up with the high command.

We shoved off in a convoy that was neither bigger nor smaller than all the others. The convoy conference was just like all the rest. The blimp and patrol planes came out as they always did and the escort vessels snapped at our heels as escort vessels always will. The sea acted up as it usually does and spray pelted our watches with all the old customary viciousness.

Still, to me it wasn't just another trip. No Navy crew is the same when it goes aboard a transport. You are protecting live cargo. Among those hundreds of men are friends and former classmates and friends of friends and they are very valuable and irreplaceable cargo and you have a different attitude toward a transport. I thought that I had done my utmost while aboard the freighters, but on the transport I found it somehow possible to increase my vigilance. While in danger areas I never left the central control station but slept there and had my meals there.

I always feel very good about equipment aboard a transport. You have everything. You have the best of equipment and the best of men. Over half my gun crew had been torpedoed and some of them twice, and they had been bombed and shelled. Two of my boys had been in the Mediterranean for almost a year, during the period when merchant shipping was taking a terrific beating. John Henry Jones, my coxun, was once under fire for five straight days, and the planes were so thick they seemed like flies. The planes were after them all day and then when darkness fell the torpedo boats came out.

"We were riding around on tons of dynamite and the machine-gun bullets would be spraying us like hail stones," Coxun Jones told me. "But our fellows worked as calmly and deliberately as if the Nazi guns were so many riveting machines. I remember one day when the planes were zooming on us and we were pumping shells with everything we had and one of our 20-mms. jammed, and the gunner called out that he didn't know what to do . . . he'd never had a gun jam before and he said he couldn't fix it.

"'Hell you can't fix it!' our officer called. 'Take th' damn thing down and see what makes it tick. You've got nothing else to do if it doesn't work.'

"The gunner grinned at that. He wanted something to do. He didn't want to sit around ducking bullets when there was no place to duck. So he sat there calmly on deck and took down the gun as carefully as if he was cleaning a watch. The dive bombers were strafing us and the bullets were whining down and spattering the decks and our own guns were setting up a hell of a racket and men were getting hit, but our gunner just kept on working.

"Then I saw him cussing and I called to ask what the matter was and he was hunting among some shrapnel scrap, pieces about the size of your fist, and he yelled: 'Those sons-of-bitches made me lose my breech pawl!'

"But he found it and put the gun together again, slipped in the ammo, and let go. The plane he had in his sights went down smoking. I don't know whether he got it or someone else did, but I'm always going to believe he did."

Then there was Coxun Roberts, who was on the Murmansk run, and they were under steady air attack for eight days. Before that they were stalked by a submarine and they got a shot at it and smashed the conning tower and when the sub tried to get away they took out after it. Finally the sub stopped to fight and they poured more shells into it. Every time they got a hit the sub went down, but it would bounce right back up again and stay there. No matter how many rounds they poured into that U-boat, it simply wouldn't sink for keeps. Their captain finally explained it. His chart showed that the sub's stern was on a reef and the bow simply bounced up and down with the shooting. So, since no Nazis came out to surrender, the captain decided the sub had shipped water and they left it there to mark the reef, which, it was concluded, was at least one instance in which the Nazis had made a contribution to the safety of navigation.

INVASION

One of the boys had been sunk off Malta. He was picked up by a British corvette and taken to the island where he was bombed continuously for five weeks. No shipping could get in or out. He was finally taken off in a British sub and he loved to tell us about the psychology of submarine crews and just how we could bait the German U-boats so that we could get a decent shot at them. We didn't try out any of the theories, but they sounded mighty interesting.

Most of the men of our crew were very young—boys who in other circumstances would have been entering college or getting their start on farms or in jobs. They hadn't yet shared fully in the stake destined for them by American democracy, but each in his own way was appreciative of the worth of that stake, and each was ready and willing to preserve the right to it for his fellows if luck turned bad and he would not be able to enjoy it himself. I remember Kenny Krupp, gunner's mate 3rd class out of Massillon, Ohio. Kenny played football for Massillon High, and he loved nothing better than to sit and talk football by the hour. But he had a feeling, too, for the grave importance of the job we're in, and what doing that job means. Just before our major fight, he wrote a letter to his mother which I saw and shall never forget. I know he will forgive me if I quote from it. His words are engraved on my mind and they tell, better than anything I can say, how our men at the battle fronts feel about this war:

"Dear Mom:

"We're in pretty dangerous waters but I don't want you to feel badly if anything should happen to me—it wouldn't be like something cut off right in the middle, for out here we're all doing a grand and wonderful job. I'm proud to be here with this crew and I feel like I'm doing what I should be doing to make it right for all of you at home. So don't worry, we'll be back soon to stay."

I was always proud when I drew up the battle bill for our transport. It looked like a bill for a fighting ship. There were forward guns port and starboard and after guns starboard and port. There was a whole line of 20-mms. and 1.1-inch and other weapons I can't talk about, strung from stem to stern. Some of those new antiaircraft pieces were really beauties. In addition to our own equipment we had aboard some of the Army's fighting gear. We felt ready for anything. The skin of our ship was no thicker than that of the *Scotty,* but what a whale of a pounding we could deal out if we had half a chance.

Mainstay of my battle bill, in addition to Lieutenant (j.g.) G. C. MacKenzie, my junior officer (not the MacKenzie of the Creek but a mighty fine officer who now has his own crew), was Woodrow Wilson Caples, bosun's mate first class, USN. Bosun Caples weighed about 110 pounds soaking wet and he was just over the Navy's five feet minimum height but he could lick his weight in wild cats. The bosun had been in the Navy for fifteen years and he knew his way about and how to handle men. He had a youngster, a girl five months old, and to hear Bosun Caples tell it the child is a paragon of all earthly and heavenly virtues. It is a fit description of Bosun Caples' capabilities to say that he could imitate some of his child's choicest grimaces at one moment and turn the men to handsomely the next without a smile showing among the entire crew. No one dared smile unless Boats did first but his big grins came so frequently the necessities of precedence were no hardship.

We were a happy ship's company. Captain Fagen, our skipper, was a veteran merchantman, six feet tall, hard as a marlinspike, and tough and hard-boiled and sentimental as they come. Captain Fagen demanded absolute, implicit and immediate obedience and when he got it, which was constantly, he was generous and understanding and quick to give the men credit for a job well done. During the air raids that caught up with us Captain Fagen was the first to have his troopship moving and the first to maneuver his vessel into position for beaching in case we were hit. Captain Fagen has steel gray hair and needlelike eyes and a voice like a foghorn and I use the comparison as a man who has listened to a good many foghorns. He received his training as a bosun on a United States battleship. He demanded strict Navy Reg conduct aboard and he kept his ship in absolute readiness for any emergency at all times. About a year ago Captain Fagen was torpedoed in the Carribean, and this experience has given him a horrendous hatred of Germans.

Whenever we were in action, Captain Fagen would stomp around on the bridge, shouting: "The bloody bastards! Let's go get us a bloody Hun!" He's a skipper after a man's own heart, and I'm sorry I'm not to sail with him again.

Major Hantsche, the transport commander, was the Army's representative aboard the *Bouncing Betsy*. He had a temper like a thermite bomb and he was violently mad at all Germans and more so at all Japs. He felt they had personally injured him since he was never able to get back to his native state of Washington to go fishing during the trout season. During action, in between issuing orders, he went about muttering: "Dammit, I wish this war would hurry up and get finished so I can go fishing." When Major Hantsche was angry he sounded like a barrel of firecrackers. No one minded his yelling, however; they just did what Major Hantsche wanted them to and nothing terrible happened to them.

We all got on very well together—Navy, Merchant Marine and Army. About 120 Army men aided us at the guns and this helped us to get well acquainted in a hurry. All the usual Army-Navy arguments came up, of course, so we organized softball teams to settle the issues as soon as we got ashore. My Navy gun crew beat everything in sight when we got to Africa—everything, that is, but the Army. They gave us a rimming. However, our boat crew trounced the ship's crew in lifeboat races. This disturbed Captain Fagen a lot, so we ran the races over again. We beat them a second time and I was afraid for a while that the captain was going to challenge me to a sculling match in order to gain himself a victory and save the reputation of his ship.

Our quarters aboard the *Bouncing Betsy* were excellent. I even had my own shower bath. The food was abundant and well prepared with a fine variety and genuine hotel service. Whoever converted the *Betsy* did an excellent job. Quarters and passageways were well located to give easy access to the guns, and the holds were compartmented and the gangways arranged in a manner to permit the troops to disembark in a matter of minutes.

4

We were running in convoy, and a very fancy convoy it was. The commodore was taking no chances with the subs, and he would signal 90-degree turns as readily as a pedestrian turns a street corner. It was the fourth afternoon out that we got our first alarm and did an abrupt turning movement out to nowhere while the escorts, their red contact pennants flying, dashed through the ranks in search of their prey. There was no confusion nor panic now. The ships marched along and did their turns like little wooden soldiers. We heard the boom of depth charges and then did another turn 90 and then another and another, and soon we were steaming over a big oil slick and we got out our forty-fives and practiced shooting at the flotsam in the water.

There was one less U-boat to pass.

It was all done so calmly and efficiently I couldn't help contrasting those early days around Cuba when we almost ran one another down because a ship in our center came up with fire in her engine room and made smoke. There was no one making smoke now, at night there was no one disobeying the blackout regulations, and we got the signals precisely right the first time. The United States Navy and Merchant Marine had come a long way in the fight against submarines since those early days. It was a victory won by careful thinking and training ashore, by careful teamwork and expert seamanship and gunnery afloat. I felt enormously satisfied when our convoy got that sub because I knew that other convoys were getting subs in the same cool, effective manner, and I knew that the Navy had won a battle that sooner or later was going to win the war.

Those Army men with us were going to win the war too. The Army really ran that ship—the Navy gun crew merely defended it—and the Army ran it in a fashion to win the everlasting approval of every man who wears blue. Soldiers joined us at battle stations, taking over their share of the work at the guns and breaking out their own battle gear. The crew, merchant sailors signed up for the duration, were a joy to see in action. They knew their jobs and carried them out with efficiency and zest.

We hard-working Navy men kept busy between alarms and alerts. All the way over, while the Army rested, we amused our soldier kibitzers with drills—gun drills, boat drills, fire drills. The fact that scores of Army troops drilled with us didn't stop their mates. To hear them we were Boy Scouts starting a fire with a couple of wooden Indians. I have never been razzed more completely, heartlessly and outrageously in my life, nor have I ever seen better gun drills. There is no finer way to get work out of a sailor than to have an Army man around telling him he doesn't know his job.

5

We went through Gibraltar at night, barely glimpsing the rock. We were at battle stations shortly afterward, for there were reports of torpedo boats about, and there is nothing a sailor likes less than a torpedo boat when he is playing host to the Army. It always seems that when a soldier gets dunked in the drink he considers it a personal affront by the Navy and when the war is over he retaliates by raising a son for the express purpose of sending him to West Point to kick the dickens out of Annapolis, come fall.

But we had no trouble and we made our way up the coast and dropped anchor in a pretty little port.

It was time then for the Army to go through its paces, and it was our turn to heckle. It may be said that we heckled some of the finest practice landing operations ever seen on the African coast. The Army is good. Gear is numbered and stowed in such a fashion, and every movement is so timed, that the disembarkation of hundreds of men proceeds with almost perfect quietness and precision. There is no more fun than sitting comfortably on the bridge while the battle talker calls packed-down soldiers to their boat stations and sends them over the side in beautifully timed movements. Observing thus, with complete objectivity, we of the Navy gun crew were in a fine position to coach and otherwise assist our comrades in khaki. The success of the final operations probably can be attributed to the excellent advice the Army got from us Navy experts on the *Betsy*.

The Army was intent on practice for a week, so we finally wearied and left them to their fun and went ashore. We still didn't know, of course, that we were not going to fill up with Axis prisoners and start home, but we were beginning to have an idea that other plans were being prepared. There was an air about the port that presaged something big.

We saw the sights of the town by day, and inspected the bars by night. There is nothing quite so diverting as conversation in a foreign bar over a glass of imitation American beer when you are thinking that perhaps tomorrow you will be getting into a scrap. The only improvement I could suggest would be genuine American brew. British beer is awful and French beer is worse, but still I guess it is the spirit of the occasion that counts. I remember one night there were six of us, representing London, Paris, Rotterdam, Singapore and Bombay, together with me from Norfolk and Sioux Falls. Everyone knew just enough English words so that we could wax maudlin about one another's countries one minute and insult one another the next. I told them about the night in Kelly's in Panama, and so we went out and looked for some Germans or Italians, but there was none about, and we went back and had some more beer. Then I spoke a few words of Russian, and we had a sententious message in

Dutch, and a swift appreciation of the wonders of the British Empire spoken in English-French, and out of it all I received an invitation to visit a British warship.

So the next night while the Army was worn out with its landing practice I went aboard the finest vessel of war I have ever visited as the guest of Lieutenant Robert Todd, formerly of New York, now of London and the Royal Navy. It was to be a formal evening, and I, who had carried my whites over half the world for a year, had of course this time stowed them at home. But I had been assured that blues were acceptable and at about 1750 a small launch called for us and carried us to the anchorage. As we neared the gangplank a great bustle was evident, and I was informed: "Honors to a visitin' foreign officer, y'know." Being guest I preceded the party up the gangway and as I neared the top the bosun's pipe began to purl and a voice commanded: "Ten . . . shun!" I was being piped over the side with side boys and all the trimmings.

Two officers met us and after an exchange of salutes we shook hands and I was escorted to the wardroom and met any number of officers each of whom insisted on buying a drink. The bar on H.M.S. was one of those little touches missing from American men-of-war. Then I was escorted on a tour of the ship and heard some great stories of the action she had seen.

We returned to the wardroom. All the British officers were dressed quite formally—white dinner jackets and bow ties. They were friendly, jolly fellows and spent a half hour telling me of some of the practices and customs of their service until dinner was called. Then we repaired to the mess. During dinner the ship's marine band played, including in its repertoire a number of American dance tunes. One young officer leaned over and said wistfully: "Bloody shame just to sit and listen to good American dances, isn't it? Now, if we were in N'York . . ." He had liked New York.

The crew of one of the smaller ships had arranged an entertainment, a radio play, which was piped to us via the ship's battle talker. The skit was a robustious satire on proverbial British calmness under fire and the officers roared at the sallies directed at them. The British who go to sea, I found, have a sense of humor as keen and broad as our own.

Following dinner, coffee and wine were served and, at a smart rap from the president of the mess, every man became abruptly silent. The president of the mess boomed out: "Gentlemen, to His Majesty the King!" We drank the toast seated. This custom, I was told, was decreed generations ago by a lanky seafaring British king who cracked his pate on the overhead when he arose for a toast.

A moment later the voice boomed forth again: "Gentlemen, the President of the United States of America!" I was prickly with thrills as I heard that tribute. We drained our glasses, and sat for a moment savoring the emotional surge that those toasts, signifying the friendliness and closeness of our two great countries, had engendered. Then we took our coffee to the wardroom and sat talking quietly of what was ahead for us, and for America and England and our allies. Then, unexpectedly, one of the officers announced they had arranged a special treat for me: ice-cold beer.

They brought me a huge tankard of ale, delightfully frosted and floating several enormous cubes of ice. I notice that the British, though they habitually drink warm beer at home, enjoyed this treat as much as I did.

At 2300, after good, swashbuckling, ale-mellowed talk in the wardroom, the party broke up, the side boys were summoned out, and I was piped over the side to my own boat. I went ashore like an admiral. Never in my life have I had more fun than those British friends showed me.

6

Two days later a British destroyer was leaving port on a little special mission and I was given an opportunity to go along. Anne always gives me the dickens for this, but I was in need of experience and no one in the gunnery business can resist those fine little turret jobs on the fighting tin cans.

There was a minor shelling mission under way, one that required an early start. I was on deck in plenty of time, and we shoved off in the middle of the night, moving down the coast. I had thought that the *Bouncing Betsy* was rough, but she was tame as a kitten compared with our tin can, which, when all is said and done, is nothing more than a big sardine box loaded with depth charges and cannon. I spent a good share of my time below, among the gadgets at central station, listening in at the little red and green devices that indicate a contact. The control room, which looks something like an instrument panel of a bomber or the switchboard of a powerhouse, is one of the most wonderful places in the world. From there, deep in the ship, you can feel out the enemy, whether he may be in the water, in the air, or even ashore. Of course, now and then you may feel out a whale and think he is a submarine. A good many innocent whales have died in this war as a result. Captain Ahab could have a field day on a destroyer.

After a time everyone grew a little tense and I went on deck to get my experience. We were in formation, strung out in a long column, and pretty soon we got a signal and cut sharply and began running in toward a coast dim in the distance. Then our guns opened up, and I hid my head in shame as I thought of the little three-inch pieces we played with on the *Betsy*.

The blasts of fire heeled the boat over about twenty degrees and a sheet of flame seemed to envelop the deck, and then explosions roared out on all sides and the guns ducked in and out of the turrets and all the while we were running up and down the coast like a scared rabbit.

Pretty soon some searchlights prodded at us from shore, and our gunners got the range and blasted some more and the searchlights went out. Then the guns ashore began to speak, but they were bad on their range and our destroyers simply paid no attention, but went back up the coast again. We could see flares ashore where the shells were striking and farther inland we could hear explosions and see fires and we knew our air force was busy.

After a while the destroyers got tired of shelling the coast and we were ready to go back, and then we got the air alarm signal.

In a moment they came over, Axis planes bent on business. The sky plotter up in the secondary control tower started calling the elevation and range and our ack-ack guns began pumping like a battery of pistons. We could follow the tracers making a curtain in the sky, and then one of the oncoming planes zooped down out of formation and began hurtling toward ground. He fell inland and burst into flame, a blaze we could still see when we were leaving several moments later.

We began zigzagging and making circles with our guns pumping and our antiaircraft guns belching flame and smoke like angry volcanoes. Then the formation came in and bombs began dropping around us. The rocket shells made the ship so bright you could see to read a book but the planes were a little hurried or something and they zoomed over us without getting any hits. They didn't come back again, which was all right with us as we were ready to leave anyway.

On the way back I discovered that things had happened so fast I wasn't sure that I had got any experience, but I had learned to have a lot of respect for those destroyer gun crews. And I knew for sure what we needed aboard the *Betsy*—one of those listening devices that would enable us to pick up whales when time got dull on a long cruise. The destroyers really have enough excitement without them.

We came back to port as unobtrusively as we had left and I never bothered to find out exactly what we had been shooting at, but I think it was an island that the Italians later left. That afternoon while the Army practiced landing operations I had a good sleep.

7

They were beginning to mass vessels in every port up and down the African coast. Of course there was no particular significance for us in that, for we knew only about our own port, but the convention we could observe seemed to be attracting an unusual number of seafaring delegates. We thought that probably something was going to happen. It is quite amazing how much everyone can know about a coming operation without really knowing anything. We figured that the push would be on soon, but on the other hand the high command might simply be giving the Axis a bad case of jitters. The thing that convinced us was the Army, which kept right on practicing. The Army didn't hold with the colored trooper who, when told to practice a parachute jump, replied he didn't believe in practicing anything you had to do right the first time. The Army intended to have it all down cold.

We were having a pretty good time haggling with the Arabs and trying to buy eggs at less than five dollars a dozen when we got word to report to our ships. The indications were that we were going back to America, but none of us V-mailed our wives or folks on the strength of it.

When we got aboard, the Army was still there and it was not difficult for us to decide that we had not brought the troops 3,000 miles just to practice and go home again. So we held some extra gun drills in port, and I re-inspected our gear for the dozenth time, and decided we were as ready as we ever would be.

We left port about four o'clock in the afternoon after some other ships had preceded us. The Army was below and the crowds ashore must have believed that we were going back to the United States after all. There were tank lighters still in port and it was quite obvious that, slow as ships like the *Bouncing Betsy* might be, they can outrun a tank lighter any day in the week. And it was obvious that nothing of much importance was going to happen without the tank lighters around. We went west to the Cape and the men in the crew grew glum, because they had lost all faith in scuttlebutt. Our homeward direction started a new flood of rumors, but the soldiers were remaining below and taking no part in them, and pretty soon we decided that the soldiers knew perfectly what was coming off and that all we would have to do was wait.

We set a course and kept steadily on it until darkness fell and then we made a hard left rudder and paced out across the Mediterranean. Pretty soon other ships began to step into our convoy, and, despite the darkness, we knew that we were in one of the biggest convoys that man has ever gathered together. The realization finally and inescapably came to us. This was it.

Most of us were rather glad. We liked security and

solid ground as much as anyone, but we had been bat-
ting around the seven seas for months, getting blown about
and rammed and shot at without a chance to get even. Now
it seemed our turn was at hand. We were scared and very
quiet. We were anxious for things to start and be over.

We went on extra alert and the Army came up with extra
guns and we were in position to throw a solid sheet of flame
at anything that might come our way. We didn't worry
much about the Italian fleet, but we were very cautious
about submarines and planes, particularly torpedo planes.
We knew that our air force was blanketing everything in
sight, but it is always possible for a stray plane or two to
get away and come scouring the seas, out of sheer orneri-
ness. We didn't want to meet any planes.

We rendezvoused with more ships, changed course, and
started on again. Then one of those quick Mediterranean
storms blew up.

Probably it was just my imagination, but it seemed I had
never seen such waves on any of the larger oceans I had
recently inspected. The *Betsy* rolled and pitched, threatening to dump our deck cargo. The wind howled and the
spray slapped into our faces and men who thought they
knew the ways of ships staggered across the decks grasping
desperately for support as each new mountain of water
tumbled over us.

But, come wind or raging seas, those convoys marched
steadily forward through the night, those great lines of ships,

numbering some 2,000 craft: warships, ocean-going landing craft, transports, tugs, subs and sub-chasers, mine sweepers and mine layers, repair ships, self-propelled gun barges, and flat, cumbersome tank lighters that had come directly across from Africa and were weathering a storm that, most certainly, under any conditions save those of dire necessity, should have kept them snug in their harbors.

It was a great movement of sea-borne traffic, a great triumph of organization, a great victory over the elements. Those convoys took the storm and kept going. Perhaps the sudden blows that swept up that week were a blessing, for they lured the enemy into a sense of security.

I thought about what was coming next as I checked the gun stations and took my watch on the bridge. There were thousands of men, of many nations and races, out on these wild seas, bent upon one objective, the hell of flame and shot that already was raging along the coast of Sicily. We were not in the initial wave. What had happened? Had the beaches been hit in the midst of the storm? Had the soft spots been found? Would we make the beachheads, or would they have more stuff than our intelligence expected and push our men back into the sea? Would the planes come? Was this to be our time? Would those defenders on the beach be any more scared than we were now?

I cannot guess of course what the soldiers were thinking. But from the few words I heard I judged they would prefer the beaches of the Nazis in Sicily to what was going on just then out there on the ocean.

Then the storm abruptly subsided and, somewhere in the black ocean, we rendezvoused again, with our advance scouts, and got our bearing. The trip in to the beaches of Sicily had entered the home stretch.

Planes were going over, our planes. Some were bound for Sicily, others were returning. We knew that those coming back had dropped their eggs, and that somewhere in Sicily there were forts and airdromes and munitions dumps and railroad terminals roaring up in flames. Some of the planes were judged to be transports that had dropped their para-troops and I envisioned dark forms, men newly landed in enemy country, stealing to their objectives through the night, supremely confident of their own prowess and the ability of their own forces to crack the beaches and come up in time; yet men ready to die if something, somewhere, went wrong. I thought that there are a lot of jobs in this war that are much less attractive than that of the Armed Guards.

Far ahead of us hell had broken loose on the beaches. Bombs exploded into the night—sharp, vicious bursts of glare that shook the earth. Tracers streaked the sky with swift-darting ribbons of light. Planes flew in very low and the burst of bombs shook the air with increasing intensity until there was a steady hammering pressure that seemed to drive into one's very brain.

INVASION

We were bringing up reinforcements and were not a part of the actual assault landing operations, and what went on was too much for any one man to witness. I have tried to think out what I saw, and what I heard on the battle talker, and what I have reconstructed from stories of my friends, to put together the landing scene that preceded our part of the battle.

Our initial assault wave was preceded by an armada of little mine sweepers that darted silently through the night, paravanes out, clearing a path for the warships. Then a destroyer ran up out of the darkness and sped to-ward the coast, followed by another and another, until it seemed there was a dozen of them. The column cut to port at 90 degrees and then, finally, things began to wake up among the defenses ashore. A score of searchlights whited balefully and great fingers of light shot out into the sea and began to explore the horizon.

Almost simultaneously there was a bedlam of noise. The guns of the destroyers all spoke at once, and kept on talk-ing. Shells screeched shoreward and hit, blasting into the night with an uproar that made the whole atmosphere shim-mer. Some of the searchlights blanked out abruptly, and then the guns ashore opened up, coughing great sheets of flame, followed by the howl of a thousand sirens. You could actually see the great projectiles of the shore guns hurled through the air. They seemed to float for a moment, and then they dropped suddenly, between the destroyers and the first line of transports.

Those flashes ashore were all the tin cans wanted. They turned loose everything aboard, and the enemy replied in lively fashion. Aboard the transports men were leaping to their stations. From one ship a landing barge crept out, a lone, tiny boat, bound for shore to mark the beach where the landing would be made. The soldiers on the ships were very quiet and calm. Only the orders from the battle talker boomed out. The Army had practiced well. When numbers were called certain gear was broken out and certain men took their appointed places, and a certain barge was made ready. It was all very orderly.

The destroyers turned and came back, again pounding the beach. A big searchlight flashed on, stabbed to seaward, and caught a tin can in its glare. The guns were pounding on both sides and shells were dropping in the path of the destroyer. Then there was a big explosion and the searchlight went out and men along the line of ships let out a cheer.

The firing now was a steady roar, one that did not abate. The first landing barge had moved up toward the beach and was lost in darkness. Then other men began to embark, thirty men, 40-mm. guns and their bazookas, those rocket shell devices that crumpled concrete pillboxes and struck terror to the hearts of the Germans.

The barges moved off and were swallowed by sea and darkness. About two hundred yards offshore they could be

putting a pattern of surface protection about us. The Army had promised there would be very few enemy planes, and the Army was one-hundred-percent right. We had not seen any. That did not prevent a sweat bath, however, every time we glimpsed a tiny sky-speck heading in our direction.

Then, in late afternoon, it was reported that there was difficulty ashore, and soon signals went out saying that an enemy tank column had been sighted, heading for the beach.

That looked like plenty of trouble, for the position of our forces at that beach was still precarious. If tanks got close enough to the beach for the guns of the ships present to afford the landing party protection it would mean that they were too close and our troops would be in danger of being pushed into the sea.

Then, in response to messages undoubtedly, but seemingly by a sheer miracle, a big British warship steamed onto the scene, and heavy shooting started far to seaward.

Those were enormous shells. They seemed to stand in the air like great balls of fire. Then they fell a little. Then they dropped, about twelve miles inland. It was uncanny shooting. The spotters had provided perfect range. That tank column never reached the beach.

Pretty soon more of our planes came over and began tearing up the hinterland. Then our troops moved on in, and it grew very quiet. All we could see were peaceful vineyards and olive groves and men unloading barges on the beach.

8

It was not until we were in the harbor, following the successful landing operations, that battle finally came to us.

During daylight hours our own planes had been going over continuously and we had put in a busy day spotting and identifying them while they were at a safe distance. Then our troops were discharged, and as darkness fell our sense of security increased, for we had not been attacked and it appeared that the enemy air force was thoroughly under control. We had approached to within bomber distance of the Italian mainland itself, but by nightfall we were too exhausted to worry overmuch about such possibilities.

At approximately 0400 I was awakened by my duty Petty Officer who said that some flares had just been dropped over near the docks. I grabbed my shoes and ran for the bridge, yelling: "Ring the buzzer! Ring the buzzer!"

All of us were sleeping at gun stations—my own cot was just under the bridge 20-mms. The battle buzzers sounded out as I was still calling orders, and all of our guns were manned in less than one minute.

It was very dark and we could see nothing, but we could hear planes diving, and then, in a few moments, we saw flares in the distance.

We had orders not to fire unless we were directly attacked

or the warships protecting the harbor opened up. Just then the destroyer alongside us let go with her ack-ack guns.

I ordered our 20-mms. to aim high and follow the tracer fire of the warships and to "let 'er go!"

Over the phones I gave the orders to the three-inch batteries. "Fuze four . . . angle sixty degrees . . . automatic fire . . . follow tracer lines from 20's and fire when you're ready."

We started shooting immediately. We were the first among the transports to begin firing, and almost at the same moment the rest joined in.

The bombers were coming high and fast. Then we saw the flash of bombs and felt a shuddering roar just to the west of us, and the battle was joined.

A second wave of planes came in, flying very low, and we were certain they were torpedo planes. Captain Fagen had our ship in motion and soon all the craft in the anchorage were moving about, seeking to present the least possible target to the enemy and to prepare for beaching if hit. The crisscross of tracers was a beautiful sight. They laced across the darkness in a high arch, like giant fingers twining. The racket was intense, and the flash of explosion lighted up the ocean.

Then the planes were over us like a swarm of insects, thirty or forty of them, darting, swooping, doing crazy turns in the half-darkness. I called the elevation and range as well as I could and we opened wide with every gun aboard.

They dived at us, roaring through the night like enormous

angry hornets, and we could see their bombs arching down. There were two near misses, between fifty and seventy-five yards, and our ship jumped as if she were a toy sailboat suddenly pushed from behind.

Down at the guns the men were shooting like mad. I heard Clancy yelling at me and as I turned I saw him fall flat and then there was an enormous roar and a rattle of explosion that sounded as if all the roman candles and sky-rockets in the world were going off at once. An ammunition dump near us ashore had been hit, and we were bombarded with strays. I ducked until the worst of the barrage was over and when I came up I saw Clancy kicking at a hot chunk of metal that hit the deck near him. He looked at me and said: "Wow!" I ordered Clancy to bring water for the crew. We had no great need of a signalman at that moment.

In a few seconds Clancy was back, picking his way across the deck. Guns pounded and shells ashore exploded and bombs flashed about us and Clancy minced up to the crews, tipping his helmet politely and shouting: "Ice-cold beer for free, gents. Ice-cold beer for free. Don't crowd. Step lively, gents. Ice-cold beer for free."

At the guns the crews were loading and firing feverishly, yelling: "Set 'em up in th' other alley! Bing th' bingah . . . win a nize new Kewpie doll! Get them planes down here, you dirty bums!"

A call came over the phones from the Number One three-inch: "Mr. Berry, we have a hang fire."

Ordnance drill flashed into my mind: ". . . if the hang-fire persists remove all men from the gun area and train in a safe direction and wait thirty minutes and then open the breech and extricate shell and throw over side."

Wait thirty minutes because the shell didn't go off? That rule didn't fit this situation, wise as it is under normal conditions. However, you can't risk blowing up your own crew by opening the breech. . . . I ordered the crew to try three more times to fire the gun and then to report back.

In a moment the report came back: "Mr. Berry, we tried three times and she didn't fire so we tossed the damn thing overboard. Shall we proceed?"

"Hell yes!" I answered, and I guess my voice told them what I felt—that they were the best doggone gun crew in the world.

They were firing again immediately and someone's guns were bringing down planes. We saw two go hurtling into the sea, and another burst into flame ashore, but the rest kept coming and all of the fireworks from the planes and ships moved over in our direction.

Below decks things were popping too. The engine room and black gang had a real workout as Captain Fagen changed course, reversed his engines and turned and twisted his ship. Down in sick bay Kenny Krupp of Massillon, Ohio, heard the call to battle stations and the gunfire and bombs and he decided that sick bay was no place for him. The doctor attempted to stop him, and Kenny yelled: "You get the hell outa the way. I got work to do."

The first I knew of it was when I saw Krupp toiling at his gun station in his pants and G.I. nightshirt. Later, after the battle, Krupp apologized to the doctor.

The fire from the guns in the harbor began to bring down planes: four, five, six, seven. They went screeching earthward with a trail of smoke and flame and the men at the guns yelled themselves hoarse and kept on pumping out shells.

We could never be sure who hit the planes and we didn't care about that so long as they were hit, but I was wishing very heartily that one would come in for our very own.

And sure enough, one German picked us out for a close run in and began coming fast. Just at that time the smoke screen the destroyers had laid around us was filling the air and I was mad at the destroyers, for I didn't think we could see to shoot our own special plane. But then he broke in through the smoke and we could see our tracers sink right into him and he cut up sharply and then turned and plummeted into the sea. I yelled that time too, and our crew on the 20's beside me started whistling and singing and I thought for one fleeting second about the report we could write on that one, but then there were more planes and we got back to business again.

The smoke and flames from the tanker and the flashes of

explosion from the munitions dump kept up a lot of excitement in our sector which seemed to fascinate the Nazis and they dived in to shell us at close range until shrapnel splattered on our decks like rain on a tin roof.

On the bridge with me we had a green crew on one of the 20-mms. They were good workers but new to the business and I had kept them near me so I could help them if there was a jam. Right in the midst of the fighting they stopped shooting. I was busy at the phones for a minute and by the time I could get to the crew they were taking down the gun in the dark to wash away powder from a ruptured shell. I could see quickly enough that those green men needed no help from me and in a few seconds they had the gun back together and firing again. There is nothing at all the matter with those endless Navy gun drills.

By this time the scene around us was something like a nine-ring circus combined with a 4-11 fire and a Fourth of July pyrotechnics exhibit. The Nazi planes kept diving at us and their shooting was getting to be pretty accurate. One of the messengers I was using was sitting on a box near me and he suddenly jumped and looked at me and I asked what happened. He pointed to a bit of shrapnel the size of a teacup that had cut into the deck within a foot of where he was sitting. The next day we saw that the entire deck was pitted with those shrapnel hits.

One of the warships saw that we were having plenty to handle and she came past us firing everything but the galley stove. The planes were quick to take up the challenge and they came in so low the shooting cut down our aerials and convoy lights. The cables fell on the bridge, knocking me down and tangling me worse than that night when the gunner knocked me off the bridge down in the South Atlantic. I was just getting up when a soldier yelled: "Duck!" and I did, forgetting for a moment that a steel deck is no place to duck. I skinned my nose and elbows and put a dent in my helmet and those were my total injuries for the battle.

Our ship was swept with machine-gun fire and the boys who got a look said the Germans practically flew through our rigging. That attack cost them another plane. When the soldier got up he grinned at me and demanded: "When in hell, sir, will the Navy learn to dig foxholes in th' decks?"

Sergeant Donnegan, of the Army's medical detachment, who was stationed at the foot of a ladder leading to the bridge, climbed up for a quick look at us. No one had been hit.

"Sir," said the good sergeant, almost hopefully, "if there is any need of first aid, I am right here at my station at the foot of the ladder." I think Donnegan must have had a worse time than any of us, for we kept busy, and he could only wait for a call if needed. It takes real guts to stay at your station in such circumstances.

We had been fighting for more than two hours and those Nazis simply refused to leave. But our men at the guns were having an absolutely beautiful time. They were completely unafraid. The boys at the 20-mms. on the bridge were whistling and singing and yelling insults at the enemy and down on the gun deck John Henry Jones was dancing a hornpipe and howling at the top of his voice every time he thought they were getting a hit. His crew was throwing shells into the gun so fast it acted like a pom pom.

I began to be worried about our ammunition, so I ran down to the main deck and grabbed off any soldiers I could find and put them to work bringing up ammo. That was dangerous business, for when the planes burst over us they seemed to scourge every inch of the deck with bullets. But they were out of bombs, evidently, and those little bursts of lead didn't worry us so much as did the prospects of fragmentation eggs or torpedoes.

Then, suddenly, the Nazis gave up the fight and left us to the dangers of the munitions dump, which was still popping off fitfully now and then. We kept shooting until they were well out of range and then the men really celebrated, yelling, hooting, singing, doing handsprings, clapping each other on the back. They were dead with fatigue, but they didn't know it. It was not until several hours later that they began to collapse from sheer weariness.

We reduced speed, maneuvered about, and returned to our anchorage. A kind of silence returned to the harbor. All we could hear beyond our own ship was the crackling of flames from the dump. Ashore we could see fires where the planes had been brought down.

I posted the watches and we broke the crew into four sections and took the Army gunners who had worked with us to chow in the Navy mess. We had a fine breakfast—eggs, bacon, cakes and coffee served up with battle talk. When we had finished, the Army men begged us to stage another air raid so that we could have another breakfast like it.

Following chow I intended to have the Navy boys secure to quarters for a rest, but, without orders from me, they went immediately back to the guns. So we cleaned them, filled the ready boxes and cleared away all the debris before a single man was ready to quit for a bit of caulking off.

We had no casualities. We have endlessly marveled at that fact, for it seemed impossible that any ship could sustain the strafing we had undergone without someone being hit. We checked all hands and no one had received more than a few scratches and bruises and those did not come from enemy fire. Krupp was declared rehabilitated after he had presented his apologies to the doctor, and even he did not go back to sick bay. We all tried to tell each other how we felt about the fight, but I guess Clarence, our colored steward, summed it up better than anyone. "Now when I gets back," he said, "I don't need to fib. Brother, I been there."

Later that day I heard that the guns from our ships, including the warships, brought down fourteen enemy planes.

9

I think that's about it for the present. I wouldn't have missed my experiences with the Navy's Armed Guard for anything in the world.

War is a senseless, terrible thing, yet, somehow, out of war come some of the finest moments a man can know. There are those who believe that teaching men to kill may corrupt their minds and hearts. That might very well be true, if killing was the only part of our job. But we are taught principles of sacrifice, devotion to duty, teamwork for the common good, that will, I am positive, overshadow our lessons in destruction.

My observation of men in common danger has taught me to love them. I have learned to appreciate the goodness inherent in us all. The task before us is like the surgeon's: We must remove the cancer to keep the body whole. It is not a pretty job. We undertake it hating not the poor, diseased tissue we must cut away, but hating only the cancer our civilization has allowed to develop.

We do not talk much about why we do the job. We simply know that it must be done.